MY FATHER THE PRIEST

MY FATHER THE PRIEST

THE LIFE AND TIMES OF THE VERY REVEREND DR. PETER SAMETZ

FOUNDING MISSIONARY PRIEST OF THE UKRAINIAN ORTHODOX CHURCH OF CANADA

WILLIAM SAMETZ

HYPERTEXT PLUS
TORONTO • CANADA
2008

HYPERTEXT PLUS
www.htplus.net
mail@htplus.net
Printed in Canada.

MY FATHER THE PRIEST
ISBN 978-0-9696700-5-6   (pbk.)

COVER PHOTO
Courtesy of the Toronto Star Archives.

LIBRARY AND ARCHIVES CANADA
CATALOGUING IN PUBLICATION

Sametz, William, 1926-
    My father the priest : the life and times of the Very
Reverend Dr. Peter Sametz : founding missionary priest
of the Ukrainian Orthodox Church of Canada / William
Sametz.

Includes index.
ISBN 978-0-9696700-5-6

    1. Sametz, Peter. 2. Ukraïnska pravoslavna tserkva v
Kanadi--History.   3. Ukraïnska pravoslavna tserkva v
Kanadi--Missions--Canada.   4. Ukraïnska pravoslavna
tserkva v Kanadi--Clergy--Biography. 5. Priests--Canada
--Biography.   6. Missionaries--Canada--Biography.
7. Ukrainian Canadians--Biography. I. Title.

BX743.9.S24S24 2008   281.9'71092   C2008-905945-X

CONTENTS

ACKNOWLEDGEMENTS

I would like to thank Wasyl Sydorenko, the editor of *Cathedral Bells*, the parish newsletter of Saint Volodymyr Cathedral, for all of the prepress work, the cover design, and final proof, that have made this book possible. What could have been a gruelling technical task became a labour of love for him. He was assisted by his lovely daughter, Natalia Sydorenko, who did the preliminary scans of all the images in the book. And special thanks to Wasyl's sister, Dr. Halyna Sydorenko, for reviewing the text.

I would also like to express my gratitude to the University of Toronto Library and the Petro Jacyk Resource Centre for their help in verifying countless historical facts, dates and details.

William Sametz

CREDITS

Most of the photographs used in this book are from the Sametz family archive. The cover photograph of Fr. Peter Sametz, as well as those on pages 190 and 223, were taken by the *Toronto Star*, but thanks to Wendy Watts of Toronto Star Archives, we have permission to use them. The photograph on page 197 was taken by the now-defunct *Toronto Telegram* and is considered to be public domain.

DEDICATION

WILLIAM CLEMENT CHEWCHUK
1987-2006

This book is dedicated to the memory of the great-grandson of the Very Reverend Dr. Peter Sametz and his wife Katherine, the grandson of William and Rosalia Sametz, the son of Walter and Gloria Chewchuk, and the brother of Katherine Chewchuk.

All proceeds from the sale of this book go to the Saint Volodymyr Foundation in memory of *Vasylko*.

ix

THE PIONEERS' PRAYER

Blessed are the meek,
*for they shall inherit the earth.**

Alone, in a new land—thousands of miles from their native Ukraine—the pioneers would go into the fields they were given to break.

But before they would plough their fields or sow their seeds, they would kneel, cross themselves, and talk to God.

They would pray to the Almighty and thank Him for all His worldly gifts—His gift of love and His gift of daily bread.

They knew they were created in God's image— and as icons of God, they knew they were to pass on His gifts of love and forgiveness to their brothers and sisters.

With life so short and fleeting, they knew that all transgressions were to be forgiven.

This Divine legacy of Christian Faith was passed on to our pioneers from generation to generation for a thousand years in our native Ukraine.

Dedicated to my pioneer parishioners,
Fr. Peter Sametz

* The Beatitudes

BOOK 1

THE PRELUDE AND INTRODUCTION

The New World
that was to become his parish

According to the grace of God given to me,
like a skilled master builder I laid a foundation,
and someone else is building upon it.
Let each one take care how he builds upon it.

St. Paul, 1 Corinthians 3:10

The Historical Setting—the New World that was to become his parish

Ukrainians came to Canada and the United States as early as the 1880s.

While passing through Burlingame, a town just south of San Francisco, during a family vacation to California in the 1960s, we stopped before a church with blue and yellow onion-shaped domes. A plaque on the front of the church identified it as a Russian Orthodox church, like many we had seen in the San Francisco area. When we entered, we noticed that the prayer books in the pews were all in the Ukrainian language. This church was one of many built to serve the Orthodox émigrés from Tsarist Russia, who came there by way of the Aleutian Islands in Alaska and down through British Columbia. Among them were many Ukrainians.

The early settlers always felt that the church was an integral part of their lives. In their newfound homeland and with their newfound freedom, they began building their churches in Canada and the United States as early as the 1880s and 1890s.

The first wave of immigrants consisted mostly of second and third sons and daughters for whom there was no chance of inheriting land or having a future of any kind back home. They came mainly from Western

3

Ukraine (Galicia or Halychyna, Bukovyna and Volyn), which was then part of the old Austro-Hungarian Empire. The borders of Russian-held Ukraine were closed and sealed to emigration. But here they would meet in their churches to pray and sing, to share their hardships and their sorrows, and to find company in their loneliness. They knew they needed their combined strength to support each other in times of need. As members of one large church family, they sought to worship God in the same manner that their ancestors had worshipped Him.

Foreign missionaries were sent to them. Belgian Jesuits and Basilians came from the Roman Catholic Church and Russian priests called "batiushkas" from the Russian Orthodox Church. Even the Presbyterian Church sent out missionaries to "Christianize" people of a nation that had already prayed to the Glory of God for nearly one thousand years.

North Atlantic Company advertisement from Western Ukraine.

The Beginnings

In March, 1891, 361 delegates of the Ukrainian Greek Catholic Church gathered at a "sobor" (church conference) in Shamoken, Pennsylvania. The delegates sent a request to the Ukrainian Greek Catholic Metropolia in Lviv, Western Ukraine, to obtain their own Greek Catholic priests to serve the new parishes of North America. In 1901, Metropolitan Andrei Sheptytsky promised to help the new parishes, but he could not get a single priest from his eparchy to give up an established, comfortable lifestyle and "volunteer" to go into the wilderness of the New World.

At that time, the Ukrainian Greek Catholic Church in Canada was under the jurisdiction of two French Roman Catholic bishops—Archbishop Adélard Langevin of St. Boniface and Bishop Émile-Joseph Legal of St. Albert. Both bishops felt strongly that it was not in the interest of the Roman Catholic Church to organize the Ukrainian Greek Catholic Church under a separate Ukrainian hierarchy. The two bishops also insisted on a celibate clergy and rejected the idea that the Ukrainian Greek Catholic Church had been allowed married priests.

The Roman Catholic bishops did not understand or have any feelings for the Rite of the Eastern Byzantine Church. In particular, they did not understand the rela-

5

tionship between religion and nationality, how the two were intertwined in Ukrainian religious life and how they established Ukrainian identity. Meanwhile, Ukrainians wanted married priests who spoke their own language and practised the same Rite they had always followed.

The Roman Catholic bishops also demanded that legal ownership of all church buildings and properties be placed into a Bishop's Trust or deeded in the name of the Roman Catholic Church. For the Ukrainian Greek Catholics this further complicated relations with the Roman Catholic Church. As immigrants, they had built their churches themselves, and with their own finances. Now they felt the Roman Catholic Church was exerting too much dominance over their lives and interfering in their affairs.

Orthodox Ukrainians from Bukovyna found themselves in a similar situation with the Russian Orthodox Church. At that time, the jurisdiction of Orthodox Churches in North America was in the hands of the Russian Orthodox Church, which was sponsored and funded directly by the Tsar of Russia. Not surprisingly, requests by the Orthodox Bukovynians for Ukrainian Orthodox priests were refused.

By 1905, nearly every Ukrainian parish in Alberta, with a desire to worship as it chose, was being torn apart by the Roman Catholic Church on one side and the

Russian Orthodox Church on the other. Both sides battled to seize church assets belonging to the settlers. It took the famous Star-Wostok Case, which went all the way to the House of Lords in London, England (the highest court of appeal at that time), to set a precedent. And it was these poor Ukrainian farm folk who set the precedent for all the people of Canada, regardless of race or creed, that it was their right to enjoy the freedom to worship as they choose and that parishioners were recognized as the rightful owners of their houses of worship.

Canada was very fortunate to have immigrants of such calibre. Ukrainian pioneers, who came to Canada, were "people of the soil." And even though they came from areas of Europe where people had been subjugated for centuries, they had a burning desire for freedom. They may not have spoken a second language or had an education, but they had their seeds of wheat that made Canada a world producer of quality grain.

The Political Environment

Nevertheless, the Ukrainians, who had come to Canada to seek a better life, were regarded with mistrust and suspicion. They were poor, they babbled in a strange language and they wore strange clothing—shawls, sheepskin coats, embroidered shirts, etc. And yet they had the strength and courage to travel halfway around the world to a strange, unsettled land in search of a better life for their children. But to many of Canada's gentry, they were the "undesirables."

In July, 1899, during a debate in Canada's House of Commons, Edward Gawler Prior (the Member of Parliament for Victoria, British Columbia) rose to speak: "I am told, by men whom I can trust, that these people are wanting in all principles of loyalty, patriotism, and cleanliness... in fact, all principles that go to fit them for good citizenship... the Galicians live under circumstances that I think, can hardly be found to exist even among the Chinese. Their manners... so I am told by men who have lived close to them for some time, are very little removed from the habits of animals." (Hansard, July 7, 1899)

These views were fostered by the Canadian gentry, who themselves were second and third sons, who had been sent out to the colonies to be rid of and to make their own way in the territories. What they did not want to admit was that everyone in Canada was an immigrant or a descendant of one. All were new to this country, except for the First Nations.

WASPish attitudes were not reserved for Ukrainians alone. The Chinese "enjoyed" the honour of paying the head tax, while they helped to build the Great Canadian Railway that bound this country from sea to sea.

The Japanese were also singled out as enemy aliens "to enjoy" the select privilege of internment during

World War II, as had 8,000 Ukrainians interned in prison camps during World War I. Ukrainians were guilty of arriving in Canada with Austrian passports of the old Austro-Hungarian Empire, which had ruled the provinces of Western Ukraine—Galicia, Bukovyna and Volyn.

Sir Wilfred Laurier's government wanted to populate and develop the prairies with homesteaders. The Minister of the Interior, Sir Clifford Sifton, advertized for immigrants, distributing over one million pamphlets with the promise of land, freedom and a prosperous future in Canada.

Sifton defended the new settlers, in answer to Prior's misguided statements, with these words: "So far as the Galicians are concerned, the attacks that have been made upon them are most unfair and more ungenerous... our experience of these people teaches us, that they are industrious, careful and law abiding, and their strongest desire is to assimilate with Canadians... So far as their general habits are concerned, I may say, that they are people who lived in poverty. That is no crime on their part. I venture to say, that the ancestors of many prominent citizens of Canada were poor in the country whence they came, and no one thinks less of them on that account. They are people of good intellectual capacity and they are moral and willing people." (Hansard, July 7, 1899)

Personal Observations

While growing up, I was also personally exposed to prejudices, barbs and misconceptions, in the many schools I attended as the son of a missionary priest. Among the choice epithets I was labelled with were "honky," "bohonk," "garlic-eater"—and these were some of the gentler terms I was exposed to. It still amazes me that my father, the priest, endowed with a five-foot-two stature, ministered as a giant among his people. He came to give them faith, to sustain them with hope and to create an identity for them.

Ukrainians had come with just what they could carry in their little straw suitcases. Although they were basically illiterate, they had an astounding natural intelligence and a burning desire to become "a somebody." Arriving as Ruthenians, Bukovynians, Galicians or Volyniaks, my father helped to give them a common identity, a feeling of self-worth and dignity. He taught them that they were all members of a great princely nation, rich in culture and mores, and with great scholarly traditions. They were all truly "born of royalty." They believed that when God created the world, he had set the lands of Ukraine for himself. They all believed that their Ukraine was one of the most beautiful lands that was created especially for them, and wherever they went,

З нагоди відзначення
100 ліття Поселення
Українців у м. Торонто

Конгрес Українців Канади
вшановує

Отця Архп. д-р ПЕТРА САМЦЯ

за душпастирську опіку та
довголітнє вірне служіння Богові,
Українській Православній Церкві й
Українському народові.

28 січня 2001

Posthumous award recognizing the Very Reverend Dr. Peter Sametz as one of the most outstanding contributors during the first century of Ukrainian settlement in Toronto.

The Very Reverend Dr. Peter Sametz at age 55 in 1948.

they brought this gift with them. They knew they had to sow their seeds in the soil that was Canada, which was now given to them, and that they were called by God to do good wherever they may be.

No priest in Canada baptized more children, married more, buried more, or influenced more people to achieve greatness than my father. Although he may not have been at the very top of the list, he certainly belongs in the top hundred of Canadians. He was truly a giant among his people, and if any Canadian deserves to be recognized for his contribution to the greatness of Canada, he most certainly does for his share.

The needs and ideals of every generation change. Indeed, change has become the common factor. Even in the 20 years since my father passed on, we have witnessed more changes in our complex society, than in the whole previous history of mankind. It is exciting to be alive today and to witness these changes. The Church and its message-givers must also change and adjust in delivering the message of Jesus Christ. Delivering a relevant message has become more difficult in today's ever-changing society. It was a much simpler task when Christ first spoke to a primitive society 2,000 years ago. Hopefully, today's message-givers will realize that faith and belief are two completely different factors, and that you cannot preach one without the other. "The Divine is truly within us!" was my father's clarion call.

Today, as I walk into any one of our churches, it is hard to find anyone who still remembers the name of the priest that performed one of the first Divine Liturgies of the Ukrainian Orthodox Church of Canada. Time passes.

Introduction to his Memoirs

While still a practising priest, at age 88, the Very Reverend Dr. Peter Sametz sat down to write his living history, describing his involvement in the social movements within the Canadian community, and the orientation, assimilation, and contribution of the Ukrainian community to the cultural mosaic of Canada.

He handwrote his memoirs in his native Ukrainian language. The initial translations into English were done by his eldest son, my brother Zenon, a renowned sociologist, professor and economic advisor to the Canadian government. These were literal and quite stilted. Before they could be completed, both my father and brother passed away. Zenon's wife, Eileen, called me several years later to ask me what to do with the pile of notes. I immediately drove to Ottawa to retrieve this material. It took several more years before I had the opportunity to look at them. In rewriting these literal translations, the life story became a biography. I have also taken the liberty to insert into these memoirs some of my own observations of my father's life.

This is not an attempt to write a formal history of the Ukrainian Orthodox Church of Canada. The late Senator Paul Yuzyk wrote "The Ukrainian Greek Orthodox Church of Canada, 1918-1951" (University of Ottawa Press, 1981) as his doctoral thesis. Dr. Odarka Trosky, in 1968, and others have done excellent work in describing this history. It is also well documented in four volumes written by the Very Reverend Dr. Semen W. Sawchuk and Prof. Yuri Mulyk-Lucyk.

I feel that a true perspective of a life in this momentous period of Canada's history cannot be obtained from studies of official historical documents, because they will not accurately reflect the spirit of events as they occurred, and it may fall victim to subjective interpretations by historians who never lived in or witnessed that period of time. This is my father's story as he wrote it and as I lived through it with him.

I have to single out the most important person in my life, my chief editor, my remarkable wife, Rose. She has been a great gift to me and she possesses incredible talent. She can spell better than her computer can spell-check. She recognizes a poor grammatical construction a mile off. "If it doesn't make sense to me, and I know what you want to say, how can anyone else get it?" This is her credo, and she is absolutely correct!

William Sametz, 2008

I have always felt that my mission was more than to pass on the teachings of the wisdom of Jesus and His Apostles. I devoted my life to give faith and hope, to inspire, and to teach my people and their children. I also felt that I had to give them dignity and identity.

I tried to teach them to love God and to love one another, the only real and true commandments of Jesus. I had to teach them to ignore the name-calling, and "to turn the other cheek." They had to be inspired to be better, and only then were they entitled to God's gift of His daily bread, and the blessings of the wonders and benefits of this new and wondrous country—Canada.

Fr. Peter Sametz

BOOK 2

FROM MY CHILDHOOD AND MY ROOTS

Where the inspiration and fire were born

In the beginning was the Word,
and the Word was with God,
and the Word was God.

John 1:1

My Childhood

I was born on Sunday, June 4, 1893, into the family of Wasyl and Maria (née Bomok) Sametz, in the village of Hleshchava, County of Terebovlia, Ternopil Oblast (Province), Halychyna (Galicia), Western Ukraine, then under the rule of the Austro-Hungarian Empire.

My birth occurred only 45 years after the abolition of serfdom in Western Ukraine (Austro-Hungary) in 1848. It was taking a long time for our people to recover and re-discover themselves after centuries of oppression. This was a period of renaissance, the rebirth of the Ukrainian nation in Halychyna. The *Prosvita* (Enlightenment) association from Lviv sent literature and history books out to the villages where those who could read would teach others. People could now learn of their famous ancestors, of Cossack Independence and of the capital city of Kyiv, the *City of Churches*, that was blessed by St. Andrew the Apostle, patron saint of Ukraine.

The people of Hleshchava soon built a *Narodny Dim* (community centre), the centre of their cultural and educational life, with a stage for theatre and concerts, reading rooms and a library. During the summer, high school students from Lviv and Ternopil would come to read, recite and talk to villagers about life in the city. Those who could not read would memorize the readings, word for word.

My father, Wasyl, was orphaned while still a young child. He had inherited a house across the street from the church and four morgs (5.7 acres) of land. He successfully courted the beautiful Maria, daughter of Michael Bomok and Anastasia Smylski. Maria's dowry of two morgs (2.8 acres) gave the young couple ownership of six morgs (8.5 acres) plus a large garden around the house.

I was christened in the parish chapel of our elderly priest, Fr. Jezierskyj. The priest wanted to name me Constantine, a name not popular with my godparents and the villagers. Here the priest's son, the newly ordained Fr. Peter stepped in. The Ukrainian Greek Catholic Church had allowed its priests to marry, as in the Orthodox Church. Fr. Peter had grown up in the village and knew all the people well. To avoid a confrontation, the young priest resolved his father's stubbornness, and that of the godparents, by saying, "Father, please note that both godfathers are named Peter, the godmothers are married to Peters, and my name is Peter, so please permit me to baptize this child Peter." Reluctantly, the elderly priest agreed to his son's rationale. His original decision was based on the mores of the church calendar—when a child is born on the Holy Day honouring a particular saint, the saint's name was to be the child's baptismal name.

Our family lived across the road from the church where my father, Wasyl, served as church elder for many years. I remember how my father and the other two

Baptismal certificate of Peter Sametz. Parents: Wasyl Sametz and Maria Bomok. Priest: Fr. Peter Jezierskyj.

21

Author William Sametz in front of the church in Hleshchava where his father, Peter Sametz, was christened.

church elders, Holovenko and Podedvorny, used to pour hot wax while making metre-long candles on a circular frame fastened to the ceiling of our house. For our family, every Sunday was a Holy Day.

When I turned 11, after completing five years of elementary school in the village, my parents sent me to the county centre at Terebovlia for one year at the Normal School. There I learned the German language in order to prepare for the Ukrainian *gymnasia* (high school) in Lviv, where I was to continue my studies and eventually become a priest of the Ukrainian Greek Catholic Church.

Lviv

In my twelfth year, I was accepted at the Lviv Gymnasia, approximately 120 kilometres away from my village, in the capital of Western Ukraine. There was a secondary (middle) school in Ternopil, only 40 kilometres away, but for centuries Lviv had been the centre of knowledge and education of Western Ukraine. The city had the famous Pedagogical Bursa (residence school) with a fine reputation for the care and excellent upbringing of its students. The *bursa* also had a famous boys choir, under the direction of Prof. Vitoshynsky, which sang on special occasions during the Divine Liturgy led by Metropolitan Andrei Sheptytsky at the Cathedral of St. Yuri (St. George), the seat of the Metropolia.

At first I lived at the *bursa*, located on Virmensky (Armenian) Street, across from the *Narodny Dim*, where the original Lviv Gymnasia was located. Later, a new Gymnasia was built in the suburbs on Leon Sapieha Avenue, together with the new Sembratovych Bursa, which accommodated approximately 200 students.

Recognizing Ukrainian loyalty to the Emperor, the Austro-Hungarian government designated this Gymnasia especially for Ukrainian students. Although Lviv was a Ukrainian city, the Poles had dominated the city from 1340 A.D. and maintained cultural and educational control over the university, the high schools, and all other educational facilities.

I remember one occasion, when I was in third form at the Lviv Gymnasia on Leon Sapieha Avenue. Fedir Mykhailiuk, a fellow student two years older and at least a foot taller, had a problem answering Prof. Martyniuk's questions and was angrily ordered to sit down. Fedir was on the verge of tears. Quivering inside, I gathered enough courage to stand up and say to the professor that he was being too strict with Mykhailiuk, because Fedir really knew his lessons, but felt intimidated. I too was promptly ordered to sit down. At the end of term, just before our summer break, the professor advised us, "Go home and help your parents in their gardens and in their fields. Read to them and teach them what you have learned." He then pointed his finger at me, "...and that little Peter

Sametz, who had the courage to stand up to me in defence of his village friend, will some day stand up in defence of our people."

In my sixteenth year, I finished my fourth form at the Lviv Gymnasia. During this form year, we were taught the history of Ukraine. The course, however, was called *History of our Native Land* taught by Oleksander Sushko, our professor of history. We could not use the word Ukraine, so *Native Land* was substituted. He lectured us about the Union of our Ukrainian Church with Rome. According to him, the Union did not serve our nation. The Union of Brest (1596) had in fact divided our nation. Neither the faithful, the clergy, the grand princes, the hetmans nor the Cossacks desired this Union. As a historian, Prof. Sushko described the pronouncements of Grand Prince Constantine Ostrozhsky in defence of the Orthodox Faith, as the True Faith of our forefathers. Prof. Sushko also expounded on the curse of Ivan Vyshensky, a XVII c. monk who cursed those Orthodox bishops that had secretly conspired with the Polish King to unite with Rome. He even read poems to us written by Taras Shevchenko that described how the Roman Catholic Jesuits razed with fire the paradise that was Ukraine. Prof. Sushko's doctoral thesis had been on the Jesuits, which established him as a true authority on this topic. He cautioned us, however, never to mention that, which he had taught us, to the chaplain of the *bursa* where we lived. He was warning us not to create problems for ourselves. These lectures disturbed me deeply.

These were turbulent and sensational times in Western Ukraine and for the students of the Lviv Gymnasia. In the spring of 1908, Myroslav Sychynsky, a university student, assassinated the Governor-General of Galicia, Count Andrzej Potocki. It was like a thunderbolt cast in the midst of a brewing storm in Ukrainian Galicia. During elections of delegates to the parliament of the Austro-Hungarian Empire, there were terrible, bloody incidents between the Ukrainians and the Poles. There were deaths of young activists like the death of university student Adam Kotsko at the hands of Polish gendarmes. There were hunger strikes by Ukrainian students at the University of Lviv demanding to have lectures in the Ukrainian language. In the village of Chernykhiv, near Ternopil, the son of a wealthy Polish landowner shot at villagers for fishing in *his* river. Many more bloody incidents occurred in towns and villages, instigated by Polish gendarmes, especially during voting by Ukrainians in support of their own Ukrainian candidates to parliament.

I remember two memorable concerts in honour of Taras Shevchenko that were held in Lviv at this time. I attended the first concert held at the Philharmonia Hall. The Ukrainian opera singer of the Royal Swedish Opera, Modest Menzinsky, sang a rendition of Shevchenko's *Hetmany*. I can still feel it in my mind, my soul and in my heart. The presentation lecture on Shevchenko was given by the famous professor of history, Mykhailo Hrushevsky, later the President of Ukraine (1917-1918) during its brief period of independence. It was a momentous concert and an unforgettable moment in my life.

The second Shevchenko concert was held by the students themselves in our new Gymnasia auditorium on Leon Sapieha Avenue. A full choir of 120 voices was conducted by Prof. Vitoshynsky. I sang in the second soprano section. At the end of the concert we sang the hymn *Shche ne vmerla Ukraina* (Ukraine will never die). Standing beside me, Prof. Martyniuk, my home room teacher, in his thunderous voice, began to sing Ivan Franko's revolutionary hymn *No longer shall we serve the Muscovites and Poles*. Our choir conductor, Prof. Vitoshynsky, was also the dean of our *bursa* and he always cared for his soloists and young singers like me.

I will always remember singing the works of Dmytro Bortniansky, the illustrious Ukrainian composer of Orthodox liturgical music, every Sunday in the Church of Preobrazhennia (Transfiguration). Dr. Stepan Fedak, a lawyer and famous defender of political dissidents, was often in attendance. Colonels Yevhen Konovalets and Andriy Melnyk, national heroes of the Ukrainian Independence Movement, were both sons-in-law of Dr. Fedak. During my final two years, I remember singing in the Cathedral of St. Yuri, in the presence of Metropolitan Sheptytsky.

The phenomenally resonant contrabass solos of Bo-banyk, one of our older students, were unforgettable. There were other soloists, my fellow villagers Wasyl Mozolyk and Marian Krushelnytsky, who later became members of the Kyiv Opera. Singing in the alto section was Wasyl Swystun, who later became a lawyer in Canada, and with others was instrumental in establishing the Ukrainian Orthodox Church of Canada. Another soloist in the second sopranos was Peter Mayevsky, who later became the priest of St. Mary the Protectress Sobor (Cathedral) on Burrows Avenue in Winnipeg. An older member of the choir, Hnat Poworoznyk, who founded Essex Packers in Hamilton, was knighted into the Order of Saint Gregory by the Pope.

During this period, my native village, Hleshchava, blossomed forth with culture, education and material prosperity. It became one of the most enlightened villages in Western Ukraine. Here I give credit to young Fr. Peter Jezierskyj, the one who baptized me, for organizing the *Prosvita* library, the Temperance Brotherhood, the theatrical ensemble, the cooperative to market produce, and *Sich,* the youth organization. The *korchmy* (taverns) and other reminders of serfdom and servitude were shut down.

The *chornozem* (black earth) of the Podil region was exceedingly fertile and village families soon bought out the lands from their aristocratic landowners. Bountiful harvests, marketed by their own cooperatives, enabled the prospering villagers to send their children to schools of higher education in Ternopil and Lviv.

Although my father had been orphaned early in life and had little formal education, he had innate managerial skills, and set out plans for the future of all his children. Fedir, the eldest son, was to inherit the lands and become the farmer of the family lands. The second son, Hnat (Ihnat), would be the tradesman, and I, Peter, the youngest, was to become a priest. When Fedir and Hnat were conscripted into the army, the farming was left to my older sister Anna and to my younger sister Justina along with my parents.

A Change in Life's Course

In my sixteenth year I told my father I could no longer continue studying for the priesthood. I told him that I would be leaving for the New World and that I would no longer be a burden to him or to my brothers and sisters. I promised him that I would never do anything to harm the respect, honour or the name of the family.

I withdrew from the fifth class of the Lviv Gymnasia, and went to Germany in search of employment. At a factory in Chemnitz, a town south of Berlin, I apprenticed with a master glassblower and was assigned to tend the annealing ovens. I earned 12 German marks a week and saved my money to pay for the journey I was planning to Canada. As much as glassblowing was an interesting and artistic vocation, it was not one that I wanted to spend the rest of my life doing. After one year I had earned enough money for my journey to Canada. I then returned to my village. I had dreamt of the freedom and the opportunity for success offered by Canada from the time my two uncles (my mother's brothers) left for Canada in 1898— Peter Bomok, at age 30, and Ivan Bomok, at age 18. I was only five years old. I recall the moment of their leaving with tears in my eyes. They had both come to bid farewell to my mother and asked for her blessing.

It was different for me when I was preparing to leave for Canada. I was not journeying somewhere unknown. I was going to join my uncles, Peter and Ivan, as well as my father's brother, uncle George. A fellow villager, and a close friend of mine, Myroslaw Stechishin, had also left for Canada earlier. My sister Anna had married into the Stechishin family, making Myroslaw a family relative. Stechishin was working in Canada as editor of *Robochyi Narod* (The Working People) and was living with his brother Michael, also my childhood friend. I remembered Michael well. At age 16, he saved his family from armed Polish gendarmes, who had burst into their home, searching for evidence of Ukrainian literature, which was forbidden. "Today is Sunday," Michael said, "and my widowed mother and I will not permit you to come in and disturb us during our prayers." This was a sterling display of the Stechishin strength and backbone.

It was on the Day of the Transfiguration, August 19, 1910, when I left my village together with my aunt's son, Michael Dzumaga, who was also my age—I had recently turned 17—and fifteen-year-old Julian Stechishin, the younger brother of Myroslaw and Michael. My father hitched up the horses and drove us 12 kilometres to the railway station in Terebovlia. I thanked my parents for their blessings, their prayers, their tears and their good wishes and we were on our way.

We travelled to the Port of Hamburg, Germany, where we waited three days for the steamship, Prince Adalbert. From my previous stint in Germany, I was always impressed with the order, discipline and cleanliness of the country. It took us 13 days to cross the Atlantic Ocean to the Port of Quebec City. Standing at the ship's rail was a necessity, not a pleasure. Many travellers had to endure severe seasickness as part of the cost of the ocean voyage.

At that time, to come to Canada without a sponsor, we each had to have a minimum stake of $25 in Canadian funds. During the journey, Julian Stechishin's $25 disappeared. The money was either lost or stolen. Luckily, I had over $60 Canadian, so I lent him his stake. A fellow traveller, also a fellow student of the Lviv Gymnasia, Michael Belegay, now a well-known wrestling champion, was travelling to Edmonton. He borrowed my drama books of Ivan Karpenko-Kary. They were never returned and I missed them later, when I was asked to prepare plays for the Canadian stage.

The vastness of the Atlantic Ocean was awe-inspiring, but the size and breadth of Canada were absolutely amazing. We got on the train at Quebec City and it seemed that we travelled forever through lands and forests that literally engulfed us. Many Ukrainian immigrants, who arrived in Canada at this time, had little practical knowledge of the English language. Since our names appeared in Austrian passports either in Ukrainian, Polish or German, they often became crudely misspelled by Canadian immigration officials. Everything depended on the level of literacy of the officer who first received them. My name was spelled Sametz, a throwback to my time in Germany and my knowledge of the German language. Many of my compatriots suffered ridicule for generations because of the crude spelling of their names and, as a result, gross mispronunciations.

Julian Stechishin travelled with me as far as Winnipeg, where he met up with his two brothers. I continued on to Dauphin, Manitoba, where I met my two uncles. My cousin, Michael Dzumaga, headed for Ethelbert, Manitoba, to join Smylski, his uncle. It was now the middle of September and we had travelled for over four weeks and come halfway around the world.

Recognition

Before I go any further, I would like to pay a deep and abiding homage to the fathers of Hleshchava and Terebovlia. They gave up their most talented sons and daughters to help build the cultural and educational mosaic of Canada. John Buchan, later as Lord Tweedsmuir, the Governor General of Canada, said to us, "To be a good Canadian, you must first be a good Ukrainian." What contribution have I made to Canada and to our people? I will let the reader decide. As an example of the contributions of the sons of Hleshchava, I will mention the Stechishin brothers. Myroslaw was a brilliant journalist, who had served as the Secretary of the Ukrainian Diplomatic Mission to Washington in 1919. He was editor of the *Ukrainian Voice*, published weekly in Winnipeg, and the ideologist of the Ukrainian Self-Reliance League (CYC) where he developed the clarion call *Self-help, Self-reliance, Self-respect, and Self-worth!* His brother, Michael, was a teacher, who became a lawyer in Saskatoon and then a learned judge. As a legal partner of the Honourable John Diefenbaker, Michael was described by the Prime Minister as a walking encyclopaedia. And as a writer, he was a literary giant. The youngest brother, Julian, my fellow traveller to Canada, became rector of St. Petro Mohyla Institute in Saskatoon, then a lawyer, a pedagogue and a

Myroslaw Stechishin, editor.
(1883-1947)

Michael Stechishin, judge.
(1888-1964)

Julian Stechishin, lawyer.
(1895-1971)

Savella Stechishin, writer.
(1903-2002)

34

famed orator. His wife, Savella, brilliant in her own right, wrote the first Ukrainian cookbook, *Traditional Ukrainian Cookery* (1957), which became the culinary bible of all Ukrainian families. She was recognized and awarded the Order of Canada in 1989. All three brothers were prominent among the original founders of the Ukrainian Orthodox Church of Canada.

There was Prof. Dr. Oleksander Kolessa, Dr. Carl Smylski, teachers Peter Budynsky and Cornelia Smylski, and the chemist, Evhenia Tokar-Ochrym. I must especially mention Dr. Peter Smylski. My grandmother (mother's mother) was Anastasia Smylski. Her brother, Mykola, also immigrated to Canada and his son became the world famous Dr. Peter Smylski, the oral surgeon who pioneered the Department of Oral Surgery at the University of Toronto and served as its first dean. His energy and support of St. Vladimir Institute in Toronto were legendary. While serving in the Canadian Army during World War II, Peter inadvertently discovered a POW camp in Italy of a Ukrainian Division of the German Army. The soldiers were to be taken back to the Soviet Union—surely to be executed. Peter approached Eleanor Roosevelt, wife of the President of the United States, who arranged for the whole Division to be transferred to safety in England. Thus, Peter was instrumental in saving the lives of over 8,000 Ukrainian men.

Author William Sametz in front of the village signpost in Hleshchava, Ukraine, in 1992.

When I had the opportunity to visit Ukraine in 1992, six months after the Proclamation of Independence, I visited my father's village, Hleshchava. First, I headed to the cemetery beside the church to look for my grandfather's grave, to pay homage and to pray.

Down the hill from the cemetery, I met a Maria Sametz, who at 97 remembered the day in 1910 when "little Peter" left for Canada. She told me of a priest who went to Canada from a neighbouring village, Fr. Isidore Borecky, who later became a bishop of the Ukrainian Greek Catholic Church and organized the Eastern Eparchy of this Church in Canada.

Maria's long-term memory was astounding. She told me about my grandfather's house, and why I could not find it. She said that during World War II the invading Germans herded all the women in the village, ages 8 to 80, whom they had abused and raped, including her two daughters, into the house where my father was born. Then the Germans torched the house, burning the women alive. Now I understood the reason for this intense hatred of Germans that still lingered half a century later.

Cemetery in Hleshchava, where many of our relatives are buried. This is the grave of my uncle, Hnat Sametz.

BOOK 3

MY NEW LIFE BEGINS IN CANADA

Be thankful for all things

We are royalty created by God
to be anybody we want to be.

He gives us strength and guidance,
and all things are possible
for those who believe.

Fr. Peter Sametz

Our Struggle Begins

After travelling halfway around the world from their native land, Ukrainian immigrants soon discovered that the *Promised Land* could be rewarding, but only after many tests of endurance and survival pushed them to their limit. When the immigrants arrived at their allotted homesteads, there was nothing but mud and bush, and wolves and coyotes wailing in the night. The new environment, the English language and Canadian customs were completely foreign to them. It was strange for each Ukrainian family to live alone, on their separate quarter section of allotted land, isolated from one another, often miles apart. They had arrived virtually penniless, scared and confused.

Bogus agents made false promises to recruit immigrants, who were ill-prepared for the stark realities they would soon have to face. And they fell prey to unscrupulous people who cheated them.

During the 1890s, political and national oppression by Russia in the east and Austria in the west, conscription into foreign armies to which they held no allegiance, and grinding poverty motivated Ukrainians to leave their homeland. Many of them came to Canada illiterate, because education had been denied them. Canada, however, held the promise of education, wealth, and liberty, if not for them, at least for their children. But first, they had to create the basic essentials of life from nothing, entirely on their own.

Initially, immigrants were unable to devote the time and effort necessary to develop the homestead. There was no money for livestock, equipment, or food beyond what could be grown in the garden. During their first years in Canada, the men would go off looking for work, while the wives and children looked after the homestead. Jobs were plentiful for strong backs, but men had to go where the jobs were. They worked on railroads, on construction projects, in the mines and lumber camps, or for wealthier farmers. For many months, while the men were away, the family was left to cope alone in a strange environment, and to face with tremendous courage and stamina the physical and psychological stresses of their isolation in the Canadian wilderness.

My Initiation in Canada

I soon discovered that the basic qualifications for me, as a new immigrant, were brute strength, a strong back, and unending endurance. Here, you start with a Canadian National railway shovel, a sledge hammer, a farmer's pitchfork, or a bushman's double-edged axe.

When I first arrived in Dauphin, Manitoba, in September, 1910, it was right at harvest time. I was instantly exposed to the true meaning of hard work. Pitching heavy sheaves of wheat, almost as big as I was, onto a hayrick, immediately guaranteed bleeding hand blisters and burning back muscles. I lasted all of two days, and verging on collapse, I earned the principle sum of $2, and a full bushel of chiding and ridicule.

I returned to my uncle, Ivan Bomok, who then found me a job on the *extra gang* repairing railway beds. I managed to earn enough money to clothe myself in preparation for my first Canadian winter. I stayed on my uncle George's farm, 20 miles southwest of Dauphin, at Ochre Lake. Here, I attended a one-room school called Halley (named after Halley's Comet) where I learned to speak and read the English language. It had to be instant, total immersion for me.

In Dauphin, I met up with my fellow countryman, Michael Stechishin, who was a teacher at that time. He asked me what newspaper I read. I told him that I read *The Working People*, where his brother, Myroslaw, was editor, and that I even read it back home in the village.

Michael told me that Myroslaw had had a disagreement with Paul Crath (Pavlo Krat) and his fellow socialists. He had moved on to become the editor of a newly established newspaper—*Ukrainian Voice*. In January, 1911, I became one of the first and youngest subscribers of this new Ukrainian paper and was one of its long-standing original shareholders.

My first three years in Canada were spent in hard physical labour on the farms and on the railroad. This was the only way I could earn enough money to further my education, and become *a somebody* in my new chosen land. During my first spring in Canada, I was hired by a young thirty-six-year-old farmer, Bill English, from Oak River. He would pay me $30 a month during the summer, and $10 a month during the winter, which included my room and board. After two summers and one winter, Mr. English took me to the bank where I opened my first Canadian bank account. I deposited the princely amount of $300, which I had diligently saved.

Then I heard that it was possible to earn more money during the winter working in the bush. So in the fall of 1912, I left for Saskatoon where I had to change trains to go on to Prince Albert. A young man approached me at the station in Saskatoon, asking me where I was going. He explained that he was a cook at the bush camp, where I was going, and that if I bought him his ticket to Prince Albert, he would hire me to work with him in the kitchen. He took my money and promptly disappeared. This was my first experience with what I later learned was called a *flimflam*.

A convoy of horse sleds left Prince Albert, taking food and provisions north towards Montreal Lake, deep into bush country, where I met my first lumberjacks. Because of my physical stature, I was never meant to cut timber, it requiring great strength and expertise to chop and saw properly. Instead, I was assigned a pair of beautiful black horses to manage. My task was to chain each log that was cut and have my team of horses drag it to a gathering area where the logs were to be loaded onto sleds drawn by a four-horse team. My pair of horses would then be hitched to the front of the four-horse team, to provide the additional starting power that was needed. Once the teams began to move the load, I would have to quickly unhook my lead team and jump to one side to quickly get out of the way. This was a time when my small size and agility gave me an advantage. Self-preservation was also a powerful motivating factor.

In the evenings, I would help the men with their household chores and then I would teach them how to read and write, and explain to them the importance and power of knowledge and learning. It also helped me pass time more quickly, leaving me no time to sit and feel sorry for myself.

By the fall of 1913 I had saved over $400. I went back to Winnipeg to renew my association with my fellow countrymen, the Stechishin brothers at the *Ukrainian Voice*, and to enrol at Wesley College in order to obtain my matriculation. I had always planned to become a teacher. The staff at the *Ukrainian Voice*, the manager—Peter Woycenko, the president—Taras Ferley, and the printers—Batitsky and the Uhryniuk brothers, all became part of my extended family. Wasyl Kudryk, who became editor, became my mentor. Although I did have a good family of uncles in Dauphin, their hands were full, and together with their own families were struggling for existence and self-preservation.

Teacher's certificate attained in 1914, within four years of arrival to Canada.

My Teaching Career Begins

From the first time I read this passage, I kept it with me always. *"Education is a companion which no misfortune can depress, no crime destroy, no enemy alienate, no despotism enslave. At home a friend; abroad, an introduction; in solitude, a solace; and in society, an ornament. Without it, what is a man? A splendid slave, a reasoning savage."*—Charles Varle

I became proficient in English, and obtained my teaching degree at Wesley College in Winnipeg. On March 11, 1914, the Manitoba Department of Education sent me out to take over Stoney Hill Public School in Janow (now Elma), 55 miles east of Winnipeg.

There were many young, single, lonely men attending school during the winter months, and then during the summer we would go out to the rural schools to teach. We would earn a few dollars, which enabled us to further our education. There was a drastic, ongoing shortage of teachers throughout the western provinces. Children could only attend school when a teacher was available. Education was key to allow children to climb the ladder of success in this new world their parents had chosen.

In Elma, the local general store was run by the Tuchtie family, which had two sons. The older son, Vladimir (Walter), was 10 years old at that time I taught him. Many

Peter Sametz as a young teacher in 1914.

48

years later, when I was assigned to the Hamilton parish in Ontario, Walter, who had become a lawyer, helped me with the legal work to obtain the valuable land for St. Vladimir Sobor (Cathedral) in Hamilton, all *pro bono*. It always amazed me how many people came forward to support me, whenever I had problems to face.

1914 was the centenary year of the birth of Ukraine's greatest son and poet—Taras Shevchenko. For Ukraine, Shevchenko is a combination of William Shakespeare and Robbie Burns. It was Taras' poems and writings that had ignited the spirit of his people, subjugated for hundreds of years. I felt that my pupils at Stoney Hill should put on a concert in honour of the great Ukrainian *kobzar* (bard), even though not all of them were of Ukrainian descent. Preparations were intense, but the concert was a rousing success. I may have overburdened little Marusia (the sister of Peter Melnychuk, who later became an ordained priest in our Church) with a long and difficult work by Shevchenko—*Topolia* (The Poplar), but she memorized the complete poem and recited it beautifully to a teary-eyed audience of proud parents and friends. Early in my teaching career I learned that my students would become the most effective teachers of our history and culture to their parents, as Prof. Martyniuk had once instructed us to be.

The audience begged for a repeat of the school concert, to be held in the larger town auditorium. For many of them this was the first time that they had become aware of the beauty of their own culture and literature. Mykola Syroidiw, the editor of the *Canadian Ruthenian*, (an organ of the Ukrainian Greek Catholic Church) was present, and I had asked him to give a short presentation on the life of Taras Shevchenko. He begged off, because he was too shy and deathly afraid of speaking in public. The chore became mine, and this turned out to be my first public appearance as a speaker. It was an exhilarating experience for me, and for the first time put me on the path to my true calling.

I mentioned before that not all of my students were of Ukrainian descent, but they all wanted to participate in the concerts and plays that, subsequently, I prepared for them. It was from 3 to 4, after regular school hours, that I taught Ukrainian language, literature, history and music to all the children who wanted to stay after hours to learn. I was amazed by how many of the non-Ukrainian children stayed for these lessons. During the winter I returned to Wesley College to complete my courses and obtain my degree.

I read in the *Ukrainian Voice* that in mid-August, 1914, there was going to be a convention of Ukrainian teachers in Winnipeg. After only four years in Canada, I was proud that as a young immigrant (I was only 21) I was accepted into the Teacher's Association. At the convention I met my fellow villager, Peter Budynsky, who was also a

Conference of Ukrainian Teachers, Winnipeg, c.1915.
Peter Sametz is standing third from the left in the front row.

teacher now. Other participants in the convention were Theodore Hawryluk (a future school inspector), Michael Luchkovich (a future Member of Parliament), the Mihaychuk brothers, Dmytro Yakimischak (a future lawyer), Theodore Marciniw and Peter Karmansky. As editor of the *Canadian Rusyn*, Karmansky mercilessly attacked our educational and cultural movement, which he associated with the editorial position of the *Ukrainian Voice*. At a time when Ukrainians were experiencing a cultural rebirth in Canada, his actions were counterproductive and unpopular with the rest of the teachers. At the convention we met, bonded and set up networking groups to continue developing our educational and cultural programs.

My first monthly pay from the Stoney Hill School Council was the princely sum of $55—the extra $5 was for performing janitorial duties after school hours. I spent my money buying my first ownership share in the *Ukrainian Voice* with $25 of my pay. I donated $10 to the Ukrainian People's Home on Burrows Avenue, and the remaining $20 was spent at John Petrushevych's bookstore for copies of the *History of Ukraine* by Mykhailo Hrushevsky, two volumes of Shevchenko's *Kobzar*, poems by Stepan Rudansky and a collection edited by Julian Romanchuk. This was the beginning of my prized library that I took with me wherever I went in Canada.

In 1913, after emerging from the offices of the *Ukrainian Voice*, I stopped to gaze into a store window at some drawings and maps. A gentleman invited me into the store to entice me to buy some lots in Port Arthur (now Thunder Bay), Ontario. He assured me that the lots would double or even triple my money. I immediately returned to the *Voice* to tell my good fortune to the manager, Mr. Woycenko, and to Jaroslaw Arsenych, then a student of law. Arsenych asked me how old I was (20 at that time). He told me that all these lots for sale were under water. He marched me back to the store and told the salesman that I was underage and that he had no right to sell me any real estate. He managed to get my money back. The lesson I learned here was that if the deal sounds too good to be true—*it is!* This lesson is still valid today.

Unfortunately, I had to learn the lesson twice. While at Wesley College, a Mr. Kharambura offered to double or triple my money, if I bought lots in the area of River Park. I gave him a cash deposit and was elated with my good fortune. I was living at the YMCA Settlement House at that time with Arthur Rose, who later became a legendary doctor in the Rosthern and Hafford areas of Saskatchewan. Arthur was the brother-in-law of Reverend James Woodsworth, the founder of the CCF Party. When I ran out of money, I informed the dean, Fletcher Argue, that I had to leave Wesley College and that I could not complete my degree. I explained to him why I had to leave and what I had done. Dean Argue marched me into the law offices of his friend, Mr. Parker, who asked me my age. Within a

Wasyl Swystun, lawyer.
(1893-1964)

week he got my money back for me, so that I could complete my schooling. The first time should have been a learning experience for me. The second time was just plain dumb on my part.

I went to visit my friend and fellow student of the Lviv Gymnasia, Wasyl Swystun. Wasyl was teaching at a school called Rak near Vonda, approximately 40 miles north of Saskatoon. He had arranged for the trustees of

PROVINCE OF SASKATCHEWAN

1915

DEPARTMENT OF EDUCATION

PROVISIONAL CERTIFICATE

This document gives the holder no authority to teach after the time stated.

This is to Certify that *Peter Sametz.*

is hereby licensed to teach in *Kotzko*

School District No. *2701* *of Saskatchewan, until* *October 31st.* *1915.*

Certificate No. *291 - 15.*

Countersigned

June 3rd 191 *5.*

Augustus J. Ball.

DEPUTY MINISTER

Walter Scott.

MINISTER OF EDUCATION

Teacher's certificate, Saskatchewan, 1915.

Adam Kotzko School to meet with me. This school was located in the heart of a colony of Ukrainian homesteaders, 22 miles northeast of Vonda. By Easter, in 1915, they were paying me twice as much as I had earned in Manitoba. The area was well developed, and although the chairman of the School Board was a francophone, a Mr. Noyer, his children learned the Ukrainian language, and even learned the prayers I taught to the children.

Most of the schools in this area had Ukrainian names—Adam Kotzko, Ruthenia, Rak, Borschiw, Svoboda, Poltawa, Kolomyia, Zalishchyky, Sokal, Sniatyn, etc. They were all located in the area between Saskatoon and Prince Albert. The principal of the high school in Vonda, Mr. Hjalmerson, an Icelander by birth, was trans-

55

ferred to Wynyard, and had invited me to live with his family, where I could study during the winter. After the school year ended that year, I returned to Vonda, where the trustees of Kiev School in St. Julien hired me immediately. I was developing a good reputation with my extracurricular courses in Ukrainian language, literature and history. The awakening of self-worth, self-respect and self-reliance became a huge wave of success in the communities around me. Schools became the centre of social activity in these areas, and the homesteaders were proud of the education their children were getting.

The First People's Convention

On August 4 and 5, 1916, on the initiative of the *Ukrainian Voice*, the First People's Convention was convened at the Strand Theatre, in Saskatoon. Speakers talked of the need to properly school and bring up children. Others discussed new methods of farming. Agronomists explained new opportunities to develop Canada's grain production potential and the importance to develop new strains of wheat adapted to the climate of Canada. For centuries, their motherland, Ukraine, was known as the *breadbasket of Europe*. The convention also set up training programs for stage productions, recognizing the importance of staged plays, as a medium for communicating knowledge, culture, and history to our people.

I participated in the development of training pro-grams for the stage. In the demonstrations I played the role of a jester in a play based on a Shevchenko poem. It was directed by Alexander Shtyk, an expatriate of mine from Terebovlia, who was also a teacher friend of mine from Kolomyia School, near St. Julien.

The convention decided to establish St. Petro Mohyla Institute in Saskatoon. The Institute would accommodate our children and provide them with access to higher levels of education available at high schools in Saskatoon and the University of Saskatchewan. The key proponents of this project were my fellow students from the Lviv Gym-nasia, Wasyl Swystun, the Stechishin brothers, the Saw-chuks, Theodore Hawryluk, Harry Slipchenko, as well as the many other participants who came from farms in the Ukrainian locales of Saskatchewan. Within a month, they arranged for the rental of a building at 116 Lansdowne Avenue in Saskatoon. The Institute was named in honour of St. Petro Mohyla, the XVII c. Metropolitan of Kyiv and Halych, famous for developing programs of religious and educational enlightenment in our mother country. I felt that we were truly blessed by having these educated teachers and communities that sought their self-determi-nation. There was no material or financial support for these nation-builders from any outside group or govern-ment agency. Teachers provided the leadership, mentor-ship and training that directed this phenomenal inner strength, which made people believe in the opportunities encountered and fuelled their desire to *stand up and be counted.*

The new immigrants brought with them a natural talent for entrepreneurial management. They also brought their love and care for one another, and their strength of faith and their love for their Church. They rejected the foreign missionaries that were sent to minister to them, because they treated a nation with a one-thousand-year-old history of Christianity as ignorant heathens. The parents—fathers and mothers—saw their children as the gifts from God that they were. And they lived very frugally, denying themselves much, in order that they could better provide for their children.

This strength of faith and love placed their children and grandchildren at the forefront of Canadian leadership—in church, community, state and world organizations. Their children have impacted all areas of politics and learning, in all vocations and professions.

The weekly issues of the *Ukrainian Voice* brought the new immigrants news and educated them. The first editor, Wasyl Kudryk (later a priest of the Ukrainian Orthodox Church), was referred to as the *Ukrainian Tolstoy* by the Minister of Press in the Cabinet of the Ukrainian National Republic, Dr. Osyp Nazaruk. It was Wasyl Kudryk who helped set the high standards for this newspaper that are still maintained today.

The Second People's Convention

The Second People's Convention was held one year later, in 1917, in a local theatre in Saskatoon. Our community was experiencing some very serious problems. St. Petro Mohyla Institute had decided to accept *all Ukrainians of good will*, including Galicians, Volyniaks, Bukovynians, Carpatho-Hutsuls and any others that wanted to come. They all came from different provinces of Ukraine, which had been divided between Poland, Romania, Austro-Hungary and Russia. The concept of an independent Ukraine was just beginning to emerge. But opposition to our new Institute came from the Ukrainian Greek Catholic clergy and their Bishop Nykyta Budka, who had been sent to Canada by Rome, a few years earlier, in 1912. Bishop Budka wrote to the directors of the Institute demanding full control of its operations, and that all of their assets be assigned immediately to his Bishop's Trust. The bishop threatened hostile action against the Institute if they didn't acquiesce immediately. This action helped unite the people against Bishop Budka, in spite of the fact that most of the people were from Galicia and members of his Church.

At a Ukrainian Greek Catholic convention later that year, which I attended with some of my fellow teachers, we noticed the presence of French and Belgian clergy in the front row. Bishop Budka was the Chair of the Presidium. He was a Ukrainian Greek Catholic bishop sent to Canada by the Pope, not by Metropolitan Sheptytsky in Lviv. His role, specifically, was to make sure that all the assets of the Ukrainian churches be signed over to the Bishop's Trust under the control of Rome. This was designed to circumvent the decision of the Star-Wostok Case, which I discuss later.

During this meeting a Fr. Krupa jumped up shouting, "There on the hill," and pointing to the location of the Institute, "is a swarm of drones, which we must drown in coal oil, and burn as in hell!" (The Inquisition comes to mind.) The irony of it all was the fact that out of 120 students enrolled at the Institute, about 20 or one-sixth were Orthodox, and the rest were the sons and daughters of Greek Catholic families. As Greek Catholics, we were thoroughly ashamed and furious at these threats, and at the mudslinging that came from our own clergy.

At the Second People's Convention, I was asked to prepare a dramatic theatrical production, as a media model for communicating and teaching our rich cultures and traditions. I had chosen Mykhailo Starytsky's *Vechornytsi*, a well-known Ukrainian comedy. Wasyl Swystun, who was then rector of the Institute, played the title role of Hryts. Mary Trach played Marusia, and Semen Sawchuk played the role of Dmytro. The role of Khoma was played by Nicholas Michasiw. Swystun, without his glasses, was extremely short-sighted, and during the play, instead of talking to Marusia, ended up talking to the wall. Taras Ferley recognized Swystun's problem and went backstage to slip Swystun his glasses, while I was nearly passing out in the prompter's booth. The audience loved every minute of this extra play within the play.

The ten-year period, from 1910 to 1920, had been exceptionally difficult for the new Ukrainian-Canadians. Apart from religious issues and church ownership problems that I have discussed here, we were now in the middle of World War I, which created many new problems for the poor Ukrainian immigrants. Most of them, like me, had arrived in Canada with Austro-Hungarian passports because Western Ukraine was then part of the old Austro-Hungarian Empire. Over 8,000 men were separated from wives and children, and interned in faraway labour camps and classified as enemy aliens. We were all treated as second-class citizens.

There was a drought on the prairies that wiped out the crops of many homesteaders, as well as the deadly plague of Spanish Flu in 1919 that destroyed thousands of lives. Public assembly and meetings were impossible, and all this compounded the problem of isolation and despair among the settlers.

A young farmer came to Cudworth, Saskatchewan, to buy materials for coffins for his wife and children, who had died from the influenza plague. On returning home, he collapsed and died. His neighbours came to make up the coffins and they buried the whole family together. My wife's sister, Wasylyna Bambuch, who had married Andrew Bodnarchuk in St. Julien, also died from influenza. This plague affected every single family. During the drought that came along at the same time as the plague, farmers dismantled the thatched roofs of their houses and barns, in order to feed their livestock. These were times when people thought that the world had completely forgotten them, and only their deep abiding faith carried them through this darkest moment of their lives.

My Loneliness and Homesickness

After eight years in Canada, following World War I, I was feeling homesick. I worried about my parents and how they were managing in their senior years. Just before the war started, my parents had intended to send me money to bring me back home. They worried how their youngest child was managing alone in a strange and foreign land, so far away from them.

My brother's son, Mykhailo, whom I had brought over to Canada in 1929, told me that my father, Wasyl, was truly helpless in his older years. He had prayed that his older sons would return from war, and that his youngest would come home from Canada. I have always felt guilty that I never went back home. Although my brothers

Peter Sametz, Ukrainian-Canadian.

did return safely from war, my father had already passed away. Two years later, my mother was accidentally injured during the construction of my brother Hnat's house and she also died before her allotted time.

My brother Hnat had a remarkably retentive mind. He was eight years older than I, and had memorized all the psalms and prayers by heart. Even at age 13, Hnat, while repairing what was needed around the house, would teach me the psalms and prayers by rote. He could calculate and do arithmetic in his head faster than I could with pen and paper. Later, he became the tax assessor for the village.

The inner strength of the villagers was the true strength of the nation. It was this inner strength that Joseph Stalin recognized as his prime threat when he ordered the Holodomor (Famine-Genocide) of 1932-1933 that destroyed over eight million Ukrainians. To imagine the scope of this catastrophic event, just imagine the sinking of the ship Titanic every day for the next 15 years. There were more than 2,700 deaths a day and Lazar Kaganovich, the *Eichmann of the Soviet Union*, was ordered by Stalin to raise the bar to 10,000 deaths a day. And in the war between Hitler and Stalin, more Ukrainians perished than the combined total of soldiers and civilians who died in all the other countries during World War II.

BOOK 4

THE BIRTH OF THE UKRAINIAN ORTHODOX CHURCH OF CANADA

When we are called to do, God is with us.
We will never fail.

It's what you do with what God gives you.

Fr. Peter Sametz

The Turning Point

1918 was a watershed year in the history of Ukrainians in Canada. Servitude would no longer be tolerated by our people, especially within the free society, which was Canada. The new clarion call for self-determination, self-worth, and identity ignited the hearts and minds of our people. It captured 65% of the teachers, who were in the vanguard of the movement. Following the lead of the teachers, came the farmers, homesteaders, workers and those in other vocations and businesses.

At the Lviv Gymnasia, I had learned from Prof. Sushko of the Union with Rome (1596), the Uniates, and the formation of the Ukrainian Greek Catholic Church by our own Orthodox bishops, who had sided with the King of Poland. The King had been seeking divine recognition for himself, but the Union had deeply divided the Ukrainian people in their Faith.

In Canada, we felt that we had been given a special gift from the Almighty. We now had the opportunity to return to the Faith of our forefathers. In 1918, Ukraine proclaimed itself as a free, independent, sovereign nation. There was no justification for us to remain divided as Galicians, Volyniaks, Bukovynians, or Transcarpathian Rusyns. We all had a common language. In a free country like Canada, we now had access to education, a common culture, heritage, identity and Faith. It was time for us to gather together and plan our future, and the future of our generations to come.

On July 18 and 19, 1918, in Saskatoon, a special convention was called. There were no priests or bishops present. The 150 delegates were all lay people, in their twenties and thirties, representing the various Ukrainian centres in Canada. They came from Fort William (now Thunder Bay) in the east, Vancouver in the west, and all places in-between. They were tired of the positions being taken by the Catholic bishops and their narrow-minded leadership. From the pulpit we were told that if we didn't conform to the wishes of the Catholic clergy, we would all be swept off the face of this earth. At the convention we resolved to end this situation with a declaration that stated, *"Let us return to the Faith of our ancestors, our Princes, our Hetmans and our Cossacks."*

The Brotherhood of the Ukrainian Orthodox Church of Canada was formed at this special convention and it was charged with laying the foundation for a new Church. The Brotherhood was entrusted to seek out worthy candidates to study theology and prepare for the priesthood. They also recognized the need to establish a canonical relationship with the world of Orthodoxy. They approached Bishop Alexander (Nemolovsky) of Winnipeg, a Ukrainian bishop in the Russian Orthodox Church. Initially, he was favourably inclined to the formation of the Brotherhood and its goal. At the Cleveland Sobor (church conference) in 1919 of the Russian Orthodox Church, Archimandrite Adam (Philipovsky), an aggressive Galician Russophile, attacked Bishop Alexander for his friendly attitude towards Ukrainians and the newly formed Brotherhood. The problem was that the new Church was to be Ukrainian, not Russian. Bishop Alexander returned to Winnipeg, and from the pulpit of a local Russian church renounced his support, protection and acceptance of the Brotherhood. When the editor of the *Ukrainian Voice* was threatened with legal charges for criticizing Bishop Alexander, there was more worry and consternation among us.

My Courtship

In the spring of 1918, as part of the war effort, all senior school students and teachers were recruited to work on farms. I *volunteered* to work near Kiev School, where I had been assigned to teach. The secretary of our School Board was Andrew Bodnarchuk. His wife, Wasylyna, was the daughter of original pioneers in that area, Andrew and Maria Bambuch of Cudworth, Saskatchewan. The Bambuch family had arrived in Canada in the 1890s. The family consisted of five daughters, four of whom were married. There was one single daughter, Katherine, who from age 12 had managed her family farm in the absence of sons and labourers during the war. I saw how efficient

Katherine Sametz (née Bambuch) at age 15.
Cudworth, Saskatchewan.

and hardworking she was. I also saw how fortunate and happy Andrew Bodnarchuk was with her sister, Wasylyna, and the wonderful family life he enjoyed. I felt that Katherine was the right one for me to share my life with. She was very pretty and had an amazing gift of insight, where she could feel the goodness in people. Katherine was born March 4, 1903, in Fish Creek, Saskatchewan, the site of the North-West Rebellion. This was several years before Saskatchewan became a province. As is our custom, I met with her parents to beg their permission to wed Katherine. It was the best decision I ever made in my life. With-

V.S. 18A—2M-3-46

GOVERNMENT OF THE PROVINCE OF SASKATCHEWAN
DEPARTMENT OF PUBLIC HEALTH
Division of Vital Statistics   B   N° 4343

MARRIAGE CERTIFICATE

This is to Certify that the marriage of

--PETER SAMETZ--   25 YEARS
            Bridegroom   Age
and   --CATHARINA BAMBUCH--   16 YEARS
            Bride   Age
which was solemnized on JUNE 13, 1918   at   CUDWORTH, SASK.

by the Reverend ANDREW SARMATIUK ....has been duly recorded
                    Officiating Clergyman

in this Department under the provisions of *The Vital Statistics Act* of the Province of Saskatchewan, and

was registered AUGUST 27TH 19 48, the registration number being 004735

Given under my hand and seal of the Department of Public Health at Regina,

this TWENTY-EIGHTH day of AUGUST 1948.

alC.M.Reed.
For Registrar General.

The marriage certificate issued in 1948.

71

The young Mr. and Mrs. Peter Sametz, June 13, 1918.
Cudworth, Saskatchewan.

out her complete support of me, I would have never achieved the success I did. Unfortunately, I never truly expressed my deep love, respect and appreciation of her life, a gift to me, until she was on her death bed. This is the heaviest burden I bear.

Our wedding took place on the Feast of the Ascension, June 13, 1918, in Cudworth, Saskatchewan. It was a quiet family wedding by Ukrainian standards. It included our new relatives that became part of my extended family. Present were the Kotelkos, the Hawryshes, the Semaks, as well as my countrymen, the Stechishins, the Bomoks and the Sawchuks.

I took up teaching at Horodenka School, named after the home town of my wife's family. The school was located across the road from the farm of my wife's parents. Andrew Bambuch was the first school trustee of this school district. After school was out at 4, and on Saturdays, I would help my wife with the farm work.

One Saturday the following year, in 1919, a car pulled up in front of Horodenka School. Harry Slipchenko, whom I had known since the First People's Convention of 1916, came to talk to me on behalf of the Brotherhood of the Ukrainian Orthodox Church of Canada. He told me about the convention in Saskatoon on July 18 and 19, 1918, and about the delegates from all the Ukrainian centres in Canada who decided to organize and build the Church of our forefathers, now that we had established ourselves as successful citizens in a free country—Canada. He told me that they had obtained the proper blessings from Orthodox authorities and the hierarchs, and were now recruiting candidates for the priesthood. Slipchenko said that Reverend Dr. Lazar Gherman, a New York City professor of theology in the Romanian Orthodox Church, had agreed to teach and prepare new candidates for the priesthood. Slipchenko reminded me that members of the Brotherhood knew of my knowledge of liturgical music and of my religious studies at the Lviv Gymnasia, which originally were to prepare me for the priesthood in the Ukrainian Greek Catholic Church in Ukraine.

Our Preparation

In the fall of 1919, at the outset, there were seven candidates who had volunteered to study for the priesthood. However, one candidate returned to his law studies, one felt he was too shy and introverted, one felt he lacked the calling and dedication required, and one returned to teaching.

Thus, there were three students left: a student of law, Semen W. Sawchuk, and two teachers, Dmytro E. Stratychuk and I, Peter Sametz. We began a program of total immersion, which was set out for us. I remember a wintry day in January, 1920. There was a knock on the door of our classroom at St. Petro Mohyla Institute. Isadore No-

The first three pioneer missionary priests of the Ukrainian Orthodox Church of Canada, 50th anniversary celebrations, July, 1968. Seated: Fr. Semen W. Sawchuk; standing left to right: Fr. Dmytro E. Stratychuk and Fr. Peter Sametz.

Isadore Novosad   *Metropolitan Germanos*

vosad, a grey-haired farmer from Meacham (40 miles east of Saskatoon) entered and was greeted by Reverend Dr. Gherman. Novosad said, "I have read in the press and I too have heard the vicious and slanderous remarks, an attempt to blacken your reputations, for what you are doing here, just for your desire to return our people to the Faith of our forefathers." Then he proceeded to take out a wad of bills from one of his overalls pockets and another wad out of the other—$1,000 in cash was handed over to Reverend Dr. Gherman. His son, Luka, and his two sons-in-law, Ivan Kvasnytsia and Onufriy Klukevych, followed suit. They had all mortgaged their farms for $1,000 each in order to support the new Church. In today's dollars, it was like mortgaging your home for $300,000, giving the money to the Church, and then taking 20 years to pay off the loan. This was one of the finest examples of generosity and commitment that I have witnessed in all my years of pastoral work.

These monies were turned over to the Orthodox congregation in Saskatoon, which was able to purchase a church from the Russian Orthodox Church. Reverend Dr. Gherman started this parish with the three of us, his theologians, as his cantors.

The part I found most interesting was when we were learning the prayers and the sacraments of absolution. Reverend Dr. Gherman taught us that in the event a Catholic was dying in the absence of a Catholic priest, we were to recognize that the Holy Sacraments of our two Churches could be administered. We were even taught the Hebrew prayers of absolution, the *barukhas* (blessings), in the event that one of our Hebrew brethren was on his deathbed and there was no rabbi available. Reverend Dr. Gherman taught us that interwoven with Christianity were all the Faiths. A brother was a brother regardless of colour or creed.

There was initial confusion over the canonical recognition of the new Church. The greatest obstacle that we had to face was that the Church was to be named Ukrainian Orthodox, and not Russian Orthodox. Reverend Dr. Gherman advised us to contact Metropolitan Germanos (Shehadi) of the Antiochian Orthodox Church in St. Paul, Minnesota. Metropolitan Germanos represented the Patriarchate of Antioch in North America. The Metropolitan was a gentle Syrian, who gladly adopted our Church under his spiritual and canonical guidance and said, "...until such time as you get your own worthy Ukrainian bishop."

As students, the three of us fervently prepared ourselves for our new missionary roles. There was a flood of letters from the faithful who were impatiently waiting for

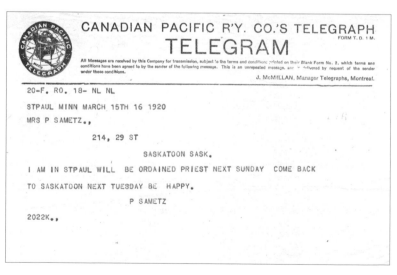

Telegram from Peter Sametz to his wife, Katherine. St. Paul, Minnesota, March 15, 1920.

our ordinations. I remember one letter from a Bukovynian named Tkachuk, who wrote to us, "You are already teachers and eminently qualified to begin serving us in our churches. We know you, and have heard you speak at our conventions. We need you now. You don't need any more learning. We have broken ties with the Russian Orthodox Church and now we need you to come to our rescue." Others wrote to remind us that Easter, the holiest day of the year, was coming soon and who would be there to give them the Holy Host, bless their Easter *paschas* (bread) and baskets. They needed us to come to baptize their children, and to marry them.

Our Ordination

We completed our studies and on March 10, 1920, the three of us, Semen Sawchuk, Dmytro Stratychuk, and I, took the train from Saskatoon to Winnipeg. In order to finance our trip to St. Paul, Minnesota, Semen Sawchuk and I had to borrow $200 from Wasyl Romanovych who worked in a store in Rosthern, Saskatchewan. Dmytro Stratychuk had saved his own money for his ordination. Semen Sawchuk had given up his opportunity to write his final exams in law. We stopped off at the offices of the *Ukrainian Voice* where, on the entrance steps, Osyp Megas (later a lawyer in Edmonton) mocked us, "Gentlemen, how are you, broke and empty-handed, prepared to battle the massive Church corporations who have bountiful resources at their disposal?" We would not allow comments like these to discourage us. All we knew was, "I am who I am. I can, I will, and I believe that I can do God's Will."

My two companions had no problems crossing the American border because both were children of parents who were naturalized citizens of Canada. I had a different problem. I had arrived in Canada in 1910, with an Austrian passport, which I still held. But the Austro-Hungarian Empire had collapsed in 1918 and the lands of Western Ukraine, where I had come from, were now ceded to post-war Poland. The staff at the Polish Consulate in Winnipeg had no idea what to do, and appeared completely disinterested in my plight. After endless delays and consultations, a secretary who spoke English, sympathized with me and took me aside to issue me a visa to cross the border.

On the train, I sat beside a chap who wore the uniform of the Canadian Immigration Service. He told me he was also travelling to St. Paul. I felt sure that his presence helped me get across the border.

I arrived at the Syrian Cathedral in St. Paul just in time to witness the ordination of my two fellow candidates into the deaconate, and then, the next day, March 13, 1920, into the priesthood. They immediately departed back to Canada. I had to remain until Sunday, March 21, to complete my ordination and to accept the Holy Sacrament of Priesthood. For my ordination, I read from the Holy Gospel the parable of the Good Samaritan. The reading was a fitting recognition of Metropolitan Germanos, who had accepted our newly-founded Church under his canonical umbrella and served as head of our Church for the first four years of its existence without receiving any monetary reward. He was truly a Good Samaritan.

I immediately wired the good news of my ordination to my young wife, Katherine, with only these words, "Be happy for us."

I found it rather curious, that on my return trip to Winnipeg, the same immigration officer happened to return with me and I found out that he had also stayed in the same hotel as I did in St. Paul. He was now in civilian clothes. I could only assume that, now that I was a priest, I no longer posed any threat and did not require any further *official attention*. Later it dawned upon me what his involvement was. For another three years after the war ended, and into 1921, when I finally received my Canadian citizenship papers, I had to report to the Royal Canadian Mounted Police detachment at least once a month. And then, every time my missionary work took me to new areas of Manitoba, I had to report to the nearest RCMP offices in advance. It was clear to me now, the immigration officer, on my trip to the United States for my ordination, was part of this surveillance.

On Sunday, March 21, 1920, the day of my ordination, the realization struck me that I had now shouldered the burden of bearing the cross that was placed on me, and my great responsibility before God and our people. Our mentor, Reverend Dr. Gherman had told us, "The birth of the Ukrainian Orthodox Church in Canada is the Will of God, and no one will defeat it. As children of God, you are called by Him to do what you must."

Peter Sametz
Border-crossing photo, March, 1920.

CLERGYMAN;S CERTIFICATE

THE UKRAINIAN GREEK ORTHODOX CHURCH OF CANADA AND THE UNITED STATES

Under the Patronage of the
Syrian Orthodox Diocese
of His Grace Metropolite
Germanos, Brooklyn, N.Y.

No. *134.*

March Earl. 9 and Wed. 22 1920

we, by the Grace of God, Germanos Metropolite of Selephkias
and Baalbek, Syria, Acting Bishop of the Syrian Antiochian Orthodox
Church in North America, and Acting Bishop of the Ukrainian Greek
Orthodox Church in Canada and the United States, do hereby certify
that Reverend Father...... *Petro Saranetz* ....
is a duly ordained priest of the Ukrainian Greek Orthodox Church in
Canada and the United States and is appointed as missionary priest
in the above named Church in Canada, with full rights to perform
the Divine Liturgy and Sacraments in accordance with the dogmas,
rites and directions of the aforesaid church, and this authorization
We certify by Our own hand and signiture.

+ *Metropolite Germanos*
....

ASSISTANT PROVINCIAL SECRETARY
R E C E I V E D

NOV 4 1938

Transferred to............................
Disposed of by............................

*Certificate of Priesthood, which was issued in both English and
Ukrainian versions by Metropolitan Germanos, March 22, 1920.*

Peter Sametz, missionary priest, 1920.

BOOK 5

THE BEGINNING OF MY MISSIONARY WORK

You are never alone in the wilderness.

We are all created in His image as living icons.

We are His children, and are created to love God and to love each other.

Fr. Peter Sametz

My First Parish, the Province of Manitoba

When I returned to Winnipeg, I stopped at the offices of the *Ukrainian Voice* to tell my dear friends that I was now an ordained priest. I then continued on to Saskatoon to join my young and patient wife, for whom I had brought some small gifts, and to join my two colleagues in order to organize our missionary work. It was decided that Fr. Sawchuk would remain in Saskatchewan and serve out of Canora, Fr. Stratychuk and Reverend Dr. Gherman left for Alberta to operate out of Suchawa, near Willingdon, and my first parish was to be the Province of Manitoba with Vita as my centre. Although Winnipeg was more central, it did not have an organized congregation.

I celebrated my first Divine Liturgy in the classroom of Shevchenko School, where I had once taught, in Vita, Manitoba, on March 28, 1920. This was my first Divine Liturgy within the Ukrainian Orthodox Church of Canada. The school overflowed with faithful who had come to sing the responses *a capella*. Fathers, mothers, and children, all joined in together, led by my *diak* (cantor), Dmytro Uhryniuk. He was ably supported by the four Bodnarchuk brothers, Nazarko, Michael, Leonty and Alex. Michael often travelled with me as my cantor, and was later ordained and became one of the finest priests of our Church. In my heart, the singing during this first Liturgy matched the singing of any cathedral. I truly felt the presence of the Lord among us and that He truly rose from the dead to live on in our souls, and that He came to help our people in their daily life of suffering, pain, and isolation, and that we would recognize His presence amongst us every day. It was very moving.

The young people of my first parish made a phenomenal contribution to the growth of our Church. Stephan Drul, Onifat Lukianchuk and John Kischuk became rectors of our new Institutes. Lukianchuk was rector of the Michael Hrushevsky Institute (now St. John's Institute) in Edmonton and the others at St. Petro Mohyla Institute in Saskatoon. What amazed me most was the respect for knowledge that people had in this parish. They understood the need and importance of higher education for their children.

In every parish that I served, women were always at the heart of it and its driving force. From the very beginning, they always took an active role in community development and in setting the standards for education at the Institutes. True leadership was exemplified by women like Mary Bodnarchuk (Symchych) from Vita and Mary Iliuk (Wawryniuk) from neighbouring Arbakka. But they only represented the tip of the iceberg.

In this area, as in many others I had served, the Ukrainian immigrants from Galicia had built their own Greek Catholic churches, while the Bukovynians had built their Orthodox churches. Basically, both Churches celebrate an identical Divine Liturgy, in spite of the split in 1596 of the Ukrainian Orthodox Church. Galician immigrants brought to Canada the Faith, which they were accustomed to in villages they left behind. But Metropolitan Sheptytsky was unable to find married Greek Catholic priests who were willing to give up their established positions, estates and holdings in Western Ukraine, and travel to an *unknown wilderness* half a world away. Meanwhile, the Roman Catholic hierarchy was not interested in setting up a separate hierarchy for Ukrainians, and could not tolerate married Greek Catholic priests in their midst.

When immigrants gathered in the churches they had built, every Sunday and Holy Day, they would pray together. Sometimes they were fortunate enough to have a cantor among them, who could sing the *Utrenia* (Matins), the psalms and the hymns as they remembered them from home. To this day I recall the great voice of a simple farmer in St. Julien as he sang during the Matins at Easter, "...as He gave His Life Eternal for us for the absolution of our sins, let us kneel before Him on this day of His Resurrection."

The church in St. Julien had refused to sign over its assets and ownership to the Roman Catholic Bishop's Trust. Before World War I, in Saskatchewan, there were two popular married Greek Catholic priests, the Rozdolsky brothers. They were forced to leave their parishioners

The young priest, Father Peter Sametz, 1920.

and Canada, because they were not accepted by the Roman Catholic Church as married Greek Catholic priests. Instead, the Roman Catholic Church sent out French and Belgian Jesuits, Basilians, and young theological students who had been taught the Ukrainian language in crash courses at special monasteries in Galicia and Poland. Here they were sent to take over the parishes built by Ukrainians. There are many coarse and bawdy anecdotes based on their gross misuse of the Ukrainian language during Church Services and their interpretive mistakes.

During my studies at the Lviv Gymnasia, I had learned that the question of authority was never an issue of religion or a matter of dogma. It was strictly an issue of power, which was derived from the early teachings of Pope St. Clement I. St. Clement propagated the existing philosophy of the Roman Caesars—*Pray, Pay and Obey*— and established this power of authority in the hands of the bishops, priests and deacons. He also preached that whoever refused to be subservient or to unconditionally obey the church leaders was guilty of insubordination to the Divine Master, Himself. Rather than uniting the Christian community, St. Clement divided the clergy and laity into superiors and subordinates. He also divided the clergy by rank.

In Canada, the politics of church power persisted. This was not acceptable to Ukrainians. But how could our faithful seek Eternal Salvation in the absence of priests and bishops? How could the poor Ukrainian home-steader, surrounded by God and all of His worldly bless-ings, and His daily presence, not recognize the true source of His divine power? They began to realize that the an-swer was *sobornopravnist* (conciliarity)—where the gov-ernance of the Church is in the hands of the hierarchy, the priests, *and the faithful.* The future of the Church was to be decided together.

The Ukrainian Bukovynians also suffered along with their Galician brothers. The Russian Synod, which en-joyed a canonical monopoly over the Orthodox Churches in Canada, forbade Metropolitan Vladimir (de Repta) of Chernivtsi, the capital of Bukovyna, from sending his Ukrainian clergy to Canada, in order to serve the Ukrain-ian Orthodox communities. Metropolitan Vladimir ap-pealed to the Russian hierarchy, but he was completely ignored. The Russians wanted to maintain exclusive con-trol over Orthodoxy in North America by claiming this right from the beginning of their missionary work in Alaska in the XVIII c. No way would they consider a sepa-rate Orthodox Church in Canada for Ukrainians. To them it was also a question of who was to be the master.

The actions of the Russian *batiushkas* (a colloquial term for bearded Russian priests) and the Roman Catho-lic hierarchy created havoc, and it was the laity who suf-fered. This situation created fertile ground for various sects and charlatans. Self-anointed Bishop Seraphim

(Stefan Ustvolsky), previously thrown out of the Ukrainian Greek Catholic Church in America, and Fr. Makarii, a self-anointed priest, had a very deleterious effect on our communities, historical beliefs and dogmas, when they tried to step into the vacuum between 1903 and 1908. They left behind a following of believers, the *Seraphims*, named after the bishop.

The faithful were ever watchful. I remember when I was in Edmonton, at a church convention in 1919. Representing the theological students was Peter Svarich, from Vegreville, Alberta, who said, "Ordinary people walk on the sidewalk, but the Russian priest walks down the middle of the road like a cow." Another time, when Belgian and French missionary priests in Ituna, Saskatchewan, could not pronounce Ukrainian words properly, resulting in vulgar meanings, many people left the church during the sermon. One old man, with his arms raised to the heavens, asked the Lord why the people were being subjected to such verbal abuse. Our people were searching for leadership. Perhaps, had there been more priests than just the three of us to serve them during this time, it would have been much easier for our people.

Vita, Manitoba

From the very beginning, Vita, Manitoba, had always been one of our leading congregations. I will always cher-

93

The original Ukrainian Orthodox Church, Vita, Manitoba.

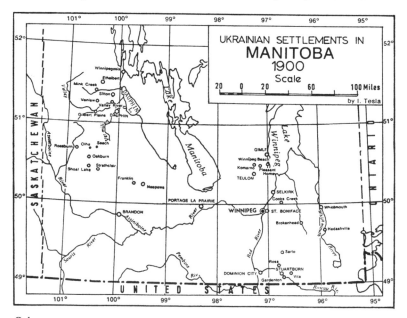

ish the altar cross, the candlesticks, and the vestments which they presented to me, and with which I served the first Divine Liturgies. I carried them with me, along with my *antimins* (altar cloth), throughout the province.

The neighbourhood congregation in Tolstoi, Manitoba, also impressed me. They had a professional *diak* (cantor), whose name was Mandziuk, who led the congregation with the responses during the Divine Liturgy. This parish was led by their teacher, Wasyl Kudryk, a lover of church music. Whenever a priest was not available, Kudryk would gather the people in the church every Sunday and they would all sing the Matins together. Kudryk later became editor of the *Ukrainian Voice*, and within three years joined our ranks of clergy.

In the first three years of serving my Manitoba parish, I served in the following communities: Vita, Arbakka, Tolstoi, Senkiw, Rosa, Dufrost, St. Norbert, East Selkirk, Sapton, Poplar Park, Ledwyn, Fraserwood, Okno, Poplarfield, Chatfield, Portage La Prairie, Kosiw, Arborg, McLeod, Sarto, Dauphin and Brandon. Sometimes I would also serve in St. Claude and in Sifton at the home of the elderly Ksionzyk and his neighbour Hupalo, who had earlier attended a Russian church.

To avoid being a burden to my farming parishes, especially at harvest time, I bought a horse and buggy, and a cutter for the winter. I would often have to travel 20 miles or so, from parish to parish. Whenever I had to go to Winnipeg, or further north to Dauphin, I would travel about 40 miles to my good parishioner Harry Bugera, about three miles from Dufrost. From there I would take the train to Winnipeg, then transfer west, or north to Dauphin to reach the adjacent areas.

The renaissance of the Ukrainian Orthodox Church, which officially began mid-July, 1918, really started much earlier. There was no clear-cut break point. Conflicts, problems, and even judicial processes haunted us for years.

Back in 1899, in Alberta, in the Star-Wostok area, about 55 miles northeast of Edmonton, our people from the Yaroslav district of Galicia had built a church. In order for a priest to be sent to serve their needs, the Roman Catholic Bishop Legal demanded the title to the church assets. During the dispute that this caused among our people, an educated farmer named Savka advised the people to write to the Russian Orthodox bishop in San Francisco for help and advice. The Russian bishop sent them a priest and his *dobrodiyka* (wife). The divisive issue of the ownership of this parish finally ended up, on appeal, at the House of Lords in London, England, the highest court of appeal in Canada at that time. The court's decision returned ownership of the church's property *to the people.* This decision established a precedent for all Canadians—churches in Canada belong to the people.

The Battle of Arbakka

Another serious church conflict occurred in Arbakka, Manitoba. In 1915, when the Russian army suffered a crushing defeat on the Eastern Front near Peremyshl (Przemyśl), the Russian priest Fr. Kobzarov, who was serving the Arbakka church, announced that there would be a special Prayer Service after the Liturgy for the health and welfare of Tsar Nicholas II and his armies.

"My good people, this Muscovite wants us to pray for the Tsar and his army, who have been murderers of our people." Nicholas Iliuk, who had the courage to stand up in church and utter these words, was charged by the priest for inducing rebellion among the people in the church.

In court, Iliuk was defended by Jaroslaw Arsenych, then an articling law student, who also acted as the court interpreter. Arsenych addressed the priest as *Fr. Katsapov* (bearded Russians and Russian priests were derisively labelled as *katsapy*—meaning *like a goat*), instead of Fr. Kobzarov. This was an interesting, provocative play on words. There was an immediate angry reaction by the bearded priest who jumped up and hollered, "Me Kobzarov, not Katsapov!" The judge wondered what was happening in his court. Arsenych apologized to the judge for his mispronunciation in the process of translation. It all sounded the same to the judge. When Arsenych again addressed the priest as *Fr. Katsapov*, the second time, the priest reacted even more angrily. The judge had enough of this display of anger by the priest in his court, and promptly dismissed the case against Iliuk.

Iliuk had taken a serious risk in challenging this Muscovite, because during World War I, Russia was an ally of Canada, against Austro-Hungary and Germany. After this legal fiasco, Fr. Kobzarov abandoned the Arbakka church and left the area. In his place, the Russian Orthodox Church sent Fr. Krehel, a priest of Ukrainian origin. During the annual meeting of the Arbakka church in 1915, the same Nicholas Iliuk made a motion that the name of the church be registered as The Ukrainian Orthodox Church of St. Nicholas, Arbakka, Manitoba. Fr. Krehel raised no objection to Iliuk's motion. This was the first church that declared itself as Ukrainian.

In the spring of 1920, I realized that I had to settle in Vita in order to more effectively serve the core of the established parishes in the south-eastern part of Manitoba. Arbakka was located about 12 miles from Vita. Today we travel 12 miles by car in a matter of minutes, but 12 miles by horse and buggy in the summer or by cutter or sleigh in the winter was a formidable challenge for me and my parishioners. At that time our only mode of transportation was horse or oxen and wagon or sleigh.

On Easter Sunday, in April, 1920, I served the midnight Paschal Service in Arbakka, and blessed the Easter *paschas* (bread) and baskets at 3 o'clock in the morning. The church was filled to overflowing. We went outside in procession with the Holy Cross and the *khoruhvy* (church banners) where I proceeded to bless the Paschal breads, meat, butter, coloured eggs and hand-painted pysanky. I am sure that it helped that I had befriended the local RCMP officer, to whom I had to report with my Austrian passport. He had driven me to the church. The presence of this huge policeman, who remained for the Liturgy, certainly prevented any potential problems from arising with the group which was opposed to my presence, which was being stirred up by the Russian priest.

Iliuk asked me to return the following Sunday for the Church Service. I travelled with him to the church and everything appeared peaceful. While Iliuk tethered the horses, I walked to the church with my valise. The church was surrounded by the *opposition* led by a huge and powerful Nicholas Goshuliak, who boomed out, "If it was Iliuk who invited you to this church today, then go to his house and conduct your Service there." Iliuk immediately entered into hot and loud discussions with the men and women present.

Fortunately a car had driven up from Vita with Nazarko Bodnarchuk and Joseph Kulachkowsky. They were two well-known and respected merchants, as well as church and community leaders, who had come to pick me up for my next Church Service, which was to be in Vita.

The Divine Liturgy was not served in Arbakka that day, but at least we avoided a serious disturbance. Oddly, Goshuliak invited Bodnarchuk, Kulachkowsky and me to dinner at his house where he declared to us, "I am not the Russophile that I appeared to be today. If Iliuk had not taken the initiative to lead the Ukrainian faction, then I would have probably stood in his place."

Of the approximately 70 families that belonged to the church in Arbakka, about 35 of the younger and more *Canadianized* supported Iliuk, and the rest followed Goshuliak. I believe that they were all jealous of Iliuk, who had become a very successful farmer, with a six-hundred-forty-acre section of land. He also owned the local general store which served as the local post office. In those days, the post office provided basic banking services for the locals, as well as the mail service.

On February 1, 1921, I was asked to perform the Holy Sacrament of Marriage for a young couple in Arbakka. I arrived at Iliuk's store, where he harnessed his horses, and on the way to church we picked up Davidiuk, the church elder. It was a brutally cold February winter day. Iliuk swept the church floor while Davidiuk set up a wood fire in the stove. I had removed my fur hat, because we were in church, and we waited for the church to warm up. Suddenly, we heard shouts from outside, "Iliuk, Iliuk, this is the last time you will bring your priest to our church!" A group of farmers in their big bear coats, which was stirred up by the Russian priest (a Ukrainian Russophile), came armed with big rocks prepared to stone us to death. Iliuk told me to run out of the church and get help from the nearest neighbour.

The mob forced Iliuk against the altar, but as they were pushing him out of the church, Iliuk tripped over the threshold, and the revolver he had taken out of his pocket, discharged. He nearly shot himself in the foot. After hearing the report of the revolver, Iliuk's assailants quickly ran off. Iliuk arose from the snow bank where he had fallen and hollered after them, "I will shoot anyone of you who will ever be bold enough to come after me!" The bridal party began arriving by sleigh and I quickly told them to go to Vita, 12 miles away, where I finally performed their Wedding Service.

Two weeks later, the RCMP arrived in Vita from Emerson, about 30 miles away, where their headquarters were located. They stopped at Kulachkowsky's store to have dinner and mentioned that they had come to arrest Iliuk on a complaint laid by the Russian archimandrite. Leonty Bodnarchuk grabbed a neighbour's horse and rode the 12 miles to Arbakka to warn Iliuk.

Iliuk commandeered Davidiuk, a great driver, to take him northeast to the railway station in order to catch the Fort Frances train to Winnipeg. In Winnipeg, Iliuk went straight to Arsenych, now a graduate lawyer, to explain his problems. Arsenych was actually happy to see Iliuk, because he had just prepared the registration of the Deed of Title for the Ukrainian Greek Orthodox Church of Arbakka. And Iliuk, as postmaster and storekeeper, took out a permit to carry a revolver. Next morning, he took the CN train 40 miles south to Dufrost, then trudged through the snow to Bugera's store. This stop I used as a transfer point, where I often left my horse, whenever I had to take the train to minister in Winnipeg and in other parts of the province.

Iliuk met me and together we went to the court house in Emerson, where the adherents of the Russian Church had laid charges of mischief against Iliuk. We hired a young lawyer, Mr. Foster, who spent an hour or so with us so that I could brief him on the history of our Church, and the problems we had encountered in Arbakka.

The Russian faction had hired another lawyer, Mr. Andrews, who wondered out loud how our lawyer knew so much about the history of our Church. Iliuk and I did not require court interpreters, but the other side was served by a German interpreter who spoke Ukrainian very poorly. Archimandrite Benjamin, together with the local priest, Fr. Biluch, represented the Russian Church. They both spoke in a dialect from the Carpathian Mountains, probably a Boyko dialect. The interpreter turned to the judge and said, "I understand Ukrainian and I understand Russian, but I do not understand the language they are using." When Judge Ashby asked the archimandrite what

In January, 2003, the rebuilt St. Nicholas Ukrainian Orthodox Church of Arbakka, Manitoba was moved to the Fort La Reine Museum in Portage La Prairie, some 200 miles away. The original church, built in 1914 was destroyed by fire in 1935 during a thunder storm. It was rebuilt in 1939.

was the nationality of his people, he promptly said, "Russian," and that he was representing, "the Russian Orthodox Church."

Immediately, the judge challenged the archimandrite stating, "There is not a single Russian among them. I have known these people since they settled in this area, from Emerson to the Ontario border, and south to the American border, and I know a lot of them personally. I know that they are all Ukrainian." The judge looked at the Deed of Title before him, that Iliuk had brought from Winnipeg, and he showed the archimandrite the official registration of the church as the Ukrainian Greek Orthodox Church of Arbakka, Manitoba. The case was dismissed.

We paid our lawyer, Mr. Foster, $25 for his services. As the three of us, Iliuk, Davidiuk and I, passed the group huddled with the archimandrite and their lawyer on our way to the station, we heard Mr. Andrews say, "Gentlemen, whenever Iliuk comes to church with his priest, don't you dare stop them or you will all be in serious trouble with the authorities."

Perhaps I have dwelt too much on the Arbakka story, but it was a prime example of the kind of struggle we had to endure in the beginning. My parishioners were all an amazing example of generosity, spirit and moral support. And this is what gave me the strength and courage to expand my mission in Manitoba.

The Mission Expands

All the existing churches demanded my services at the same time, especially at the Great Feasts of Easter, Christmas, and Jordan (Epiphany). I was very fortunate, and I thank the Good Lord that He blessed me with a most supportive and understanding young wife, who was working hard in the cafeteria of St. John's College in Winnipeg and supported me financially. Many of the parishes could not offer us any support. The costs of travel, room and board, seemed overwhelming. Although I believed that the Good Lord would always provide, I was thankful to my wife for her support.

In my missionary work, there were many small churches that I served. There were many times when I had to bring my cross, the two candelabras and my *antimins* to serve the faithful in their homes or in schools, community centres and town halls. I had previously listed some of the earliest congregations and parishes of our Church in Manitoba, but there were many, many more parishes operating out of private homes. Once, on the spur of the moment, while perusing the map of Manitoba with Fr. Sawchuk, he asked me how many parishes I served. I counted up to 29 before we stopped.

In 1921, the people from Transcona begged me to serve them on Palm Sunday, and to bless their willows.

The church was new, large, as yet unfinished, but it was filled to overflowing. The willows were lined on two walls of the church and during the blessing of the willows, as I swung the metal sprinkler of Holy Water, the head flew off into the willows. The church elder had to dig it out of the willows to end an awkward moment for me. After the Service, the president of the parish approached me and said, "Father, if you return next Sunday to bless our Easter *paschas* and baskets, the church is yours." The church was Ukrainian Greek Catholic, but had not yet been incorporated. Their Catholic bishop had vowed, "Though I lose half the parishes in Manitoba, I will never allow the Transcona church out of my hands." Unfortunately, I was scheduled to serve Vita and the surrounding parishes and I was unable to include Transcona on my tour of Easter Services. Later, a new Orthodox church arose in Transcona, where regular Church Services are held to this day.

The first Orthodox church in Manitoba was located in the town of Gardenton, which subsequently became the mission centre for south-eastern Manitoba. Today, nothing remains of the Russian Orthodox Church anywhere from Winnipeg to Emerson, and from the American border to as far north as the Ukrainian settlements extended. The entire eastern part of Manitoba came under the jurisdiction of our new missionary Church—the Ukrainian Orthodox Church of Canada.

On one of my visits to the offices of the *Ukrainian Voice*, in late 1920, Peter Woycenko, the manager, introduced me to Fr. Ivan Kusey, a priest from the jurisdiction of the Polish Independent Church, then under Bishop Markevich. This bishop was sympathetic to the rebirth of our Ukrainian Orthodox Church of Canada. Earlier, when I had encountered the bishop on a train, he said to me, "Ukrainians must always be grateful to Taras Shevchenko, because it was Taras who had prepared the foundation for an independent Ukrainian state." The bishop told me that Fr. Kusey always carried the *History of Ukraine* and the writings of Shevchenko together with his Bible. He always taught his parishioners, who were located north of Winnipeg, *who they were*, and was working, as I was, to give our people self-worth and identity.

I was emboldened to approach Fr. Kusey to apply to our Consistory for acceptance in our ranks. I told him that I would immediately write to Fr. Sawchuk, who was serving as church administrator, and that I would personally endorse him. On his acceptance, Fr. Kusey was immediately assigned Alberta as his mission. Fr. Stratychuk had requested to return to the organized parishes in the Goodeve and Canora areas of Saskatchewan. This forced me to take over Fr. Kusey's parishes in Manitoba, in addition to the 23 parishes I was already serving. With Dauphin 178 miles away, it all made for a lot of exhausting travel, either by horse and buggy or by train.

Once I received a visit from a young theology student from Alberta, Stepan Hrebeniuk, a former teacher whom I had met previously at the Teacher's Convention in 1914. He came from Suchawa where Reverend Dr. Gherman had continued to teach a small seminar on theology and had prepared him for the priesthood. Hrebeniuk asked me to take him to St. Paul, Minnesota, where Metropolitan Germanos was waiting to ordain him. As we were both still waiting for our Canadian citizenship papers, we were forced to go to the Polish Embassy and beg for visas.

I harnessed my horse Shpak (starling) and headed over to Iliuk in Arbakka to get help. We were travelling at night over hard packed snow and I depended on Shpak, who knew the road better than I did. Shpak, however, turned right instead of left, and before I realized what had happened, we were already over the American border. We returned to the crossroads and backtracked to Iliuk.

With Iliuk anything and everything was possible. While I returned with Shpak to Vita, Iliuk harnessed his grey horses, and took young Hrebeniuk across the border to his friend in Lancaster, Minnesota, who then brought him to the Syrian Cathedral in St. Paul. After his ordination, now as Fr. Hrebeniuk, he retraced his steps back to Iliuk where I greeted our new priest. I had him join me to serve the parishes in my mission over the Holy Days of Christmas and the Feast of Jordan. Fr. Sawchuk then appointed Fr. Hrebeniuk to Canora, Saskatchewan.

When Fr. Kusey left for Alberta, and Reverend Dr. Gherman returned to New York City, I was left alone with my original parishes south of Winnipeg, as well as Fr. Kusey's northern parishes. I decided to relocate to Winnipeg for more effective coverage of all of these parishes. Now there was a new development of parishes in the Kosiw area located about 15 miles southwest of Dauphin, near the Riding Mountains.

Shpak (Starling)

Shpak, my special horse, deserves my commendation for his contribution to my wellbeing. In snow or sleet, Shpak never let me down. He may not have been the most beautiful specimen of a horse, but he made up for it with his horse sense. One wintry Saturday evening, while driving westward from Vita, night-time caught up with us about nine miles from Stuartburn. I turned north towards the Senkiw area. The moon was out and Shpak knew the road. I saw sleigh tracks off to the left of the road, and when I turned Shpak in that direction, we ran into a haystack in the middle of a field. We got stuck in the deep snow around us. I unharnessed Shpak to let him have some hay and to rest. It was a major task to reharness a horse in deep snow, and then lead him back to the hard-packed snow of the road from where we had originally wandered.

Shpak bobbed his head at me, signalling that he knew the road north from here, and then gave me an extra bob to show that he excused me for my bad judgement. The mocking wails of coyotes in the background accompanied us for the next two hours. When we arrived in Senkiw, Wasyl Smuk, the postmaster, was more concerned for Shpak, who had delivered me safely, than for me and my ordeal. This did not exactly boost my ego. I served the Liturgy on Sunday. After the luncheon I returned with Shpak along the same road to Vita, but now by daylight I let Shpak *do his job*. It was my challenge to Shpak's instincts that had led us astray.

When the temperature dropped, it wasn't easy to travel even by day. I would often get out of the sleigh and run behind it to keep warm. Another lifelong lesson that I quickly learned was to run in front of the horse, instead of behind him, because a horse can always run faster than you can. Shpak would sometimes stop and look back at me, waiting for me to catch up to him. And just as I would come near, he would take off again. With a great deal of begging on my part, he would relax his pace and allow me to climb back into the sleigh, exhausted.

I learned to avoid lengthy trips that would carry me into the night. Whenever I travelled west to Stuartburn, my closest parishioner, Didiychuk, would put me up for the night, and we would rest Shpak. One winter morning, Didiychuk's son Paul harnessed a pair of horses to a large grain sleigh to drive us to church across the frozen Rousseau River. After the Divine Liturgy, we seated ourselves back in the sleigh to return home for dinner. Although the horses were blanketed while they stood outside during the Service, they took off running to warm themselves up. From the high river banks, the road descended down to the river. In spite of Paul's tremendous ability and strength, he could not hold back the horses. When they reached the river, the team turned abruptly to the left, whipping us off the sleigh onto the frozen surface of the river near a large rock jutting out of the ice. The horses continued on without us, and did not stop until they returned home to their stable. Didiychuk's sixteen-year-old son immediately turned the team around, retraced their path, and found us as we sat shivering in the snow. Distances mean nothing today, with cars and good roads, but believe me, 12 miles back to Vita in a one-horse sleigh was a long distance.

My Mission Continues

After Fr. Kusey left for Alberta, I had an extra 20 parishes to serve. The good people of Vita gave me tremendous support, and took pride in the fact that they were not alone. The whole Province of Manitoba was coming together into our new Ukrainian Orthodox Church. The Vita parish took special pride, that the gift of altar cross and candlesticks they had originally presented me, was being used everywhere I went, throughout the Province.

To say that travel at that time was inconvenient is a huge understatement. Once, when I was returning from Dauphin by train, our passenger car derailed. It happened, fortunately for us, on fairly level ground. We had to wait several hours before a rescue train was dispatched to take us on to Winnipeg.

Before Easter, in 1921, I visited my mission centres and private homes, beginning north of Winnipeg at Okno, Arborg, Tudor, the Dragan family and the Zelenetskys at Winnipeg Beach. On Holy Thursday, with a severe cold, I ended up at Arnaud, the CPR station south of Winnipeg. On the train, I had mentioned to one of my parishioners, a Mrs. Tofan, that I was to be met by Michael Chubay. The elderly Mrs. Tofan was met at the station by her children, who had come by wagon to pick her up. When the stationmaster doused the lights, my driver as yet was nowhere in sight. The Tofans offered to take me to Chubay, so I put my valises in their wagon and we took off into the mist, rain and darkness.

The horses suddenly stopped and a voice boomed out, "Have you seen the priest?" The Tofans answered, "He is with us!" Chubay then bellowed, "Don't let him step in the mud. I will come alongside so he can step into my democrat (buggy)." As the democrat came alongside, Chubay's horse bolted out of its harness and took off,

Church of Sts. Peter and Paul, Kosiw, Manitoba.
First Service after completion and Official Dedication, 1921.

leaving the democrat in the middle of the road. Chubay told the Tofans to continue, as I unloaded my valises in the mud. Chubay headed on foot to a neighbour he knew, for help. He returned with a team and wagon and hitched the democrat to the wagon, with me still sitting in it. We arrived at Chubay's farm wet, cold, muddy, but safe.

I think I experienced more adventures during my first three years as a priest in Manitoba, than at any other time of my life. My sufferings were minimal when I compare them to the hardships and extreme loneliness that my people lived through. But it was truly their profound faith that kept me going, and most of the time without any financial reward. In the morning Chubay woke me, and after breakfast drove me to his brother Mykyta's home. Mykyta's son Nazarko took me the rest of the way to my parishes around Vita, almost 20 miles away.

Our Church did not have much luck in attracting clergy from the old country. The exception was Reverend Dr. Gherman, who had helped us when we needed it most. In the beginning, Reverend Dr. Gherman helped us out by serving in Suchawa, Alberta, with Fr. Stratychuk. Then Reverend Dr. Gherman went to serve in the Canora District of Saskatchewan until he was recalled by his bishop to New York City.

We had Reverend Dr. Nicholas Kopachuk, a priest from Bukovyna, who had come to take Reverend Dr. Gherman's place. It didn't take him long to discover how difficult missionary work was, with little or no financial compensation. He soon left us for the Ukrainian Greek Catholic Church in America. It turned out for the better, both for him and for us. I had tried to acquaint him with our people in Winnipeg, and even took him out to the Bukovynian parishes in the Luka and Onut communities. He could not communicate effectively with his own people when he stood up to speak, and proved to be a disappointment. Certainly, he did not have the fervour of a Nicholas Iliuk of Arbakka, a fellow countryman of his.

In the fall of 1922, I went to visit my good friend Woycenko at the *Ukrainian Voice*. He introduced me to Fr. Wasyl Novosad and his wife, who had just arrived from Chicago with plans to settle in Canada. I couldn't reach Fr. Sawchuk to consult with him. So, I took Fr. Novosad and his wife with me to Vita. I hired a young chap, who owned an automobile, to help us tour the communities of Vita and Tolstoi, to meet the parishioners. We then served the Divine Liturgy together in Vita.

I was no longer alone in Manitoba. I left Fr. Novosad in Vita. He would cover the south-eastern part of Manitoba, while I took charge of Winnipeg and northwest to Dauphin. I was now looking forward to the expansion of our missionary work.

During the first week of November, 1922, Fr. Sawchuk visited my wife and me at the home of Joseph and Mary Bohonos, where we were living at that time, and expecting the birth of our first child. My wife, Katherine, worked at St. John's College cafeteria at the University of Manitoba. She was only 19 and had already saved the princely sum of $500. It was her wish to have our first child born in a hospital. The Church had no money, and I admit that I told Fr. Sawchuk, at the Consistory meeting, which had just been held in Yorkton, about the money she had saved. Fr. Sawchuk pulled out a promissory note, signed by the members of the Consistory, which was made out for $500 and an 8% interest rate. The Church needed this money to send Fr. Sawchuk to Europe, to meet with Prof. Ivan Ohienko, and to consult with him and with Metropolitan Dionizy (Waledinskij) of Warsaw, head of the Ukrainian Autocephalous Orthodox Church of Poland (Polish Orthodox Church), about the possibility of getting a bishop to come and serve us in Canada.

My mother gave me the promissory note six weeks before she died on August 21, 1982, making me promise never to redeem the note. $500 compounded annually at a rate of 8% for 60 years, with money doubling approximately every 10 years, made the note redeemable for almost $375,000. Needless to say, my older brother Zenon was born on Sunday, November 12, on the kitchen table at the Bohonos home on the day of his Patron Saint, Zenobios. The original note was presented to Metropolitan Wasyly (Fedak), to be placed in the Church Archives, but

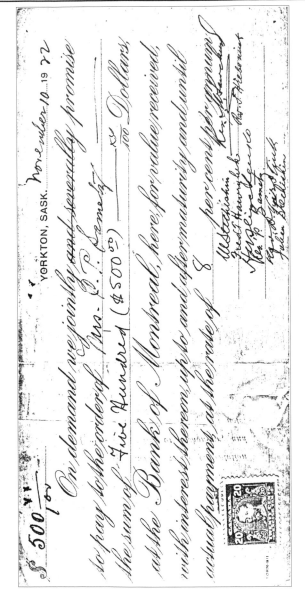

The promissory note dated November 10, 1922—two days before the birth of Zenon Sametz. Today, in 2008, the promissory note would be worth nearly $375,000.

the note has not been seen or heard of since. Zenon ended up okay. He became an associate professor at the University of Toronto, Department of Anthropology, at age 22, and later an economic adviser and Deputy Minister to Dr. O. J. Firestone in Ottawa during World War II. He helped set up the Department of Reconstruction for the Honourable C. D. Howe. He was also asked to be the Deputy Minister of Community Planning and Social Development for the Province of Newfoundland for Joey Smallwood when Newfoundland joined Canada. And he co-authored the Economic Geography of Canada with Professors Pierre Camu and Ernest P. Weeks. Being born on a kitchen table didn't seem to harm him.

November 12, 1922, was a joyous day for us. There was the birth of my first son, Zenon. Our administrator, Fr. Sawchuk, was off to Europe seeking a bishop for our Church. I had another priest, Fr. Novosad, to help me in Manitoba. And I had celebrated the Divine Liturgy in Winnipeg on a Holy Sunday.

After the Liturgy, two Ukrainian Greek Catholic priests came to me as emissaries of Metropolitan Sheptytsky. The Metropolitan of Lviv had just completed a missionary tour of Ukrainian Greek Catholic parishes in Canada, and had sent for me. He wished to meet with me at Union Station in Winnipeg. The Metropolitan knew that I had sung in the choir at his Cathedral of St. Yuri, when I was a divinity student at the Lviv Gymnasia. He knew of my new role as a missionary priest of the new Ukrainian Orthodox Church of Canada. But, after a few minutes together, he blessed me to continue the work that I was doing on behalf of our people in Canada.

When I returned home, Bohonos told me to go with him to the Ukrainian National Home (community centre) where people were celebrating the centre's first anniversary, and I was supposed to lead them in prayer. From the very beginning and right to the very end, my personal life always took a back seat to my missionary life. Besides, Bohonos told me, I would just be in the way at home. His wife, her mother, and a Mrs. Yundak, a practising midwife, were all looking after my wife and newborn son very well. Even Mrs. Yundak quietly ordered us not to be in their way.

In January, 1923, I had to go to Kosiw, in the Dauphin area, to serve the Divine Liturgy, and then perform the Holy Sacrament of Marriage for Dmytro Romanchych, who was marrying the sister of Wasyl Sklepowych, a teacher friend of mine. Dmytro Romanchych, whom I had met before at our conventions and Church Assemblies, was one of the original participants of the Saskatoon Convention of 1918, which had organized our Ukrainian Orthodox Church in Canada. Without rest, I travelled 178 miles by train to Dauphin, and then 18 miles southwest to the church in Kosiw. To me, at that time, this church was one of the most beautiful I had served at, and I could feel the deep sincerity with which the people prayed during the Divine Liturgy.

After the Liturgy, we performed the Holy Sacrament of Marriage, with the father of the bride, Fedir Sklepowych, as cantor. Although the wedding celebrations continued long after the wedding dinner was over, Dmytro Romanchych, with his team of horses, again drove me back to the railway station, 18 miles away. I was anxious to get home. At that time, we were living on a farm in Tolstoi. My newly-born son, Zenon, was ill with whooping cough, and the nearest doctor was in Emerson, many miles away.

As I sat in the station, worried, deep in thought, and buried deep in my fur coat, the lack of sleep finally caught up with me. I was so sound asleep that I didn't hear the train arrive at 3 o'clock in the morning, or change locomotives at this division stop. Before I awoke, it had already departed. I had to spend another 24 hours in deep anxiety and mental anguish, waiting for the next train to arrive and take me on to Winnipeg.

From Winnipeg I took another train to Emerson, which was almost on the American border. Then I transferred to Tolstoi. At the station I was met by Hnat Galushka, the church elder and uncle of Fr. Kudryk, who informed me of a telephone call from the Zhoda area. A young couple was waiting for me to marry them. When I told Galushka that my newborn son Zenon was ill, and that I had to go home, Galushka admonished me, saying that I was no doctor, and reminded me of my responsibility as a priest. He told me that my son was being properly looked after by the local midwife, who had all the necessary salves and prayers, and he assured me that my son would soon be better.

Before I knew it, I was back on the train to Vita, where my cantor, Michael Bodnarchuk, took me in for the night. The following day we went by sleigh to Zhoda, and then on to Dorosh. I set up an altar with my cross and candlesticks, and my *antimins*, in a home readied for the Divine Liturgy. After the Liturgy, I performed the Holy Sacrament of Marriage for the young couple.

Together with Michael Bodnarchuk, I returned to Vita, where again I spent the night. The next day, a blinding snowstorm prevented us from taking the horses out of the barn. But I was determined to get home to my wife and sick son. Carrying my valises, Bodnarchuk and I trudged on foot to the train station. At the post office, in Kulachkowsky's store, I learned that the train had already left, but was stuck in a snow bank up the line. By this time, I was truly distraught with worry for my sick son. I left my valises at the post office, taking only my vestments, and covering my head, I left on foot, southwest towards Tolstoi, about 18 miles away. I stopped in Gardenton, where the section hands sat sheltered from the storm. They would have helped me with their motorized track cart, but the cart couldn't handle the wind and the massive drifts of snow.

I continued on foot, every gap of my clothing filled with snow. About three miles from Tolstoi, one of my parishioners, Kraynik, happened by in his enclosed (hut-like) sleigh and recognized me. After a good Ukrainian admonition, he picked me up and took me to Dolynchuk's store. They served me a hot cup of tea and were shocked to hear that I had trudged 15 miles through this blinding snowstorm. Kraynik then drove me to the Galushkas, where we were staying, and I finally saw my wife and my two-month-old son.

Change always seemed to be a constant factor in my life. I remained in Tolstoi waiting for Fr. Sawchuk to return from Europe. Upon his return, Fr. Sawchuk decided to make Winnipeg the administrative centre of our Church and he moved there. The Consistory reassigned Fr. Novosad to the Wakaw-St. Julien area of Saskatchewan, to take Fr. Sawchuk's place. And after Easter, in 1923, I too was reassigned, replacing Fr. Hrebeniuk in the Canora area of Saskatchewan.

BOOK 6

MY WORK IN CANORA SASKATCHEWAN

Our God of Love will guide us, lead us, provide for us, and sustain us.

Fr. Peter Sametz

Canora, Saskatchewan

Canora had an Orthodox church, which was built by Ukrainians, and served by Fathers Kokolsky and Zazuliak, both Ukrainian, but attached to the Russian Orthodox Church. Fr. Zazuliak recognized that his Bukovynian and Galician flock overwhelmingly favoured the new Ukrainian Orthodox Church, so he quietly removed himself and left the Canora district. I took over serving this church, and until today this parish remains the stalwart of the Central Eparchy of Saskatchewan.

If all the priests of Ukrainian origin, who were serving in the Russian Orthodox Church, had come over to unite with us at that time, all would have been hailed as our pioneer heroes. Fathers Y. Ulian, T. Kysiliuk and F. Kernitsky were the only ones who initially had the fortitude to come over and join us. The others found the financial cushion provided by the Russian Orthodox Church too tempting to walk away from. They received subsidies guaranteeing them at least $100 a month, from funds transferred to Canada by the Russian Tsar's Missionary Fund. Meanwhile, our parishes could barely support a priest with about $40 a month.

After World War I, however, when the Tsar's funds dried up, the Russian Orthodox Church rapidly began to disappear. The Canora district was growing very quickly.

There was a small church 12 miles northeast of Canora, at Swidow, across from Mohyla School, which had been closed for several years. My missionary work in Manitoba, and now in Canora, had exhausted all of our personal finances. To support my family, I went back to teaching, first at Dniester School, southwest of town among the Stratychuk families, and then at Mohyla School, in Swidow. This school had one large classroom, accommodating 80 students from grade 1 to grade 8. The older children helped me with the younger children. There was a small house that we had moved into, next to the church and school. The children were from many different ethnic backgrounds, but I never had any difficulty teaching them. This allowed me to continue with my missionary work in the district, by horse and buggy.

My new travelling companion was Pete, the name of my new horse, a peaceful and gentle animal. Pete's only problem was that he could never let anyone pass him. Once, when I had to go to Kosiw in Western Manitoba, my wife, Katherine, and my three-year-old son Zenon drove me to the railway station in Canora. From there, I left for Dauphin about 120 miles away. As my wife and son left to return home in the midst of a cold winter, Pete kept a steady pace of about six miles an hour. When a Doukhobor farmer tried to pass them, by slapping the sides of his grain box sleigh, Pete took off as if he were scalded, and dumped both mother and son into a snow

Dormition of St. Mary Church near Canora, Saskatchewan.

bank. Fortunately, the farmer who had originally sold the horse to me, happened by and stopped Pete, my runaway horse, and drove mother and son back to our home.

I planted 40 fir trees around the church and school, and I understand that they still stand. Locally, they are referred to as the Sametz *sosny* (pine trees). The parish in Swidow grew. The church was expanded and repainted. About 65 families formed a faithful congregation, singing the Liturgy beautifully, and hoping for Church Services at least every second Sunday. A local farmer, Semen Tremback had a great basso voice, and as cantor led the congregation in active participation during the Service. Responses are an integral part of the Service. They are sung by the faithful, who in this manner participate in the Divine Liturgy.

I remember one occasion when Fr. Radkevych, a Greek Catholic priest serving in Antoniw, six miles west of Swidow, was having a great deal of trouble with his congregation singing the responses. He asked my cantor, Tremback, to come and help him. The Ukrainian Greek Catholic Mass is basically identical to the Orthodox Liturgy, and has remained practically unchanged since its acceptance by the Union of Brest (1596). Of course, I allowed Tremback to help. *They are also our people.* In spite of the conflicts between the Catholic and Orthodox Churches, both Churches dogmatically recognize each other's Holy Sacraments.

From Canora, in Saskatchewan, I still had to serve the Kosiw area near Dauphin, in Manitoba. My fellow villagers from Terebovlia, Western Ukraine, had built a beautiful new church. Passing through Dauphin, I met a dear friend of mine, Peter Melnychuk (I was the best man at his wedding in July, 1914), who was working there for a law firm. Peter was very well-educated, and a student of theology. I asked Peter to recall the words of the mother of St. John Chrysostom to her son, over 16 centuries earlier, "Why are you working as a lawyer in a small office? With your talents, as a priest, you would have the world to talk to, all for God, the Church and your Country!" We pray in the words of St. John Chrysostom, who wrote our Divine Liturgy hundreds of years ago, when there was still one Church, before the Great Schism of 1054.

I have always thanked the Good Lord that Peter Melnychuk listened to me. Peter became a great priest in our Church, serving the Canora, Yorkton and Wakaw areas, after I had moved on. Later Peter was called to St. John's Cathedral in Edmonton, where he prepared the Sunday School manuals for our Church. When he had become a priest, he subsidized his missionary work by working as secretary-treasurer in neighbouring municipalities, as well as teaching school east of Yorkton.

In order to help our cantors, choirs and the faithful to pray during the Divine Liturgy, Fr. Sawchuk decided to audit and print a new prayer book for our Church called *The Good Pastor*. He turned to his original priests, Fathers Sametz, Stratychuk and Melnychuk, for the money required to print the new prayer book. All three of us were still *poor as church mice*, but we all scraped together and donated the several hundred dollars needed for the initial printing. The original Ukrainian Prayer Service books that we used had been edited by Prof. Ivan Ohienko in Poland, but they were unavailable in Canada. Later, in 1952, when Prof. Ivan Ohienko became Metropolitan Ilarion of our Church, he blessed the publication of the fourth edition of *The Good Pastor*.

In the summer of 1926, Fr. Kornylo Kirstiuk came to see me in Canora. The rent for his manse in Regina was in arrears, his pay was poor and he could no longer sustain his family. His children were truly suffering from hunger.

I was not surprised by his plight. Our people, who lived in the larger cities, had no manual trades or language skills, and were usually at the bottom of the economic ladder. On the other hand, my parishioners were all becoming self-sustaining farmers, so I offered Fr. Kirstiuk my parishes. They were his countrymen from Bukovyna and Galicia, and I convinced him to take my place. I gave him $50 to cover the cost of moving his family to Canora. I knew that Fr. Hrebeniuk was to be posted to Saskatoon, and that his parishes in the Goodeve-Ituna area would become available to me.

Off to Goodeve and Ituna

In the middle of August, my family and I left the area of Mohyla School. We covered the distance of about 12 miles to Canora by horse and buggy, and then another 30 miles to Yorkton. There I left the horse in a livery stable, while we spent the night at Michael Stechishin's home. My countryman, Michael, was now a lawyer.

In the morning, I set off alone on the final 50 miles southwest to Goodeve. Along the way I stopped at a farmhouse for a sheaf of oats for my horse and to get proper directions. I was awestruck at the sight of endless fields of grain, which stretched as far as the eye could see. In the wind, it was like watching a sea of rolling waves—an amazing sight. I arrived in Goodeve that evening.

My young wife, now with two small children, arrived by train from Yorkton. Three-month-old William, who was born at Mohyla in Canora, became very ill. Everyone was busy with the harvest, but I prevailed upon a kindly Polish chap, who had a car (a rarity then), to drive us to the area hospital in Melville, where I left mother and the sick child. Zenon and I returned home by car. I could not thank this kind man enough, and after I paid him his car expenses, I made up my mind that buying a car was an absolute necessity for me. The following year, in 1927, I purchased my first automobile, a blue Essex sedan.

Fr. Kirstiuk was endowed with a marvellous singing voice. In the fall of 1926 he came to Goodeve to give a concert. It was mainly a Ukrainian audience, and he was received very well. At his second concert, in Ituna, everyone came, and I mean everyone. There were our parishioners, as well as our Greek Catholic brethren, and the English and Jewish people. I acted as the English interpreter of the words in the Ukrainian songs for the audience. Considering everything, this concert was truly an operatic affair.

The following summer, in 1927, our new Archbishop Ioan (Teodorovich) came with his pastoral visitations from Philadelphia. Everyone greeted him with great joy. Young men dressed up like Cossacks, mounted on horses, led the processions to the churches, where everyone for miles around came to see and greet our new archbishop.

Fr. Peter Sametz, Archbishop Ioan (Teodorovich) and Fr. Peter Melnychuk, Saskatchewan.

They welcomed him with tears of joy and happiness, and were enraptured by his sermons.

I proposed to the archbishop, that we also visit Fr. Kirstiuk and the Canora district. When the archbishop and I arrived in Canora, we discovered that Fr. Kirstiuk had left our Church in Canada for greener pastures in the United States. Fr. Dmytro Seneta, from Edmonton, was sent to replace him. The parish in Canora had now built a new church in town, together with a manse for the priest. Fr. Seneta also had a great voice. He was a good orator, and a talented choir conductor. Unfortunately, within a year, he too headed south to the United States.

This southward flow of our new priests—those who had joined us—affected the pace of our Church's development. Perhaps I was not gifted with an exceptional voice or special oratory talents, but I certainly fed off the depth of faith of my parishioners, who provided me with the motivation to do my missionary work and perform the Church Services our people required. It was the people who built the churches. They were the ones who came to pray. All I felt I had to do was come and serve and help direct their prayers.

Canora had been a good parish for me, but Goodeve was even more generous. They provided my family with a residence. Where other parishes would pay me $10 or $15 for a Service, Goodeve paid me at least $25. I had purchased a new car by this time, which I drove during the summer. I also had a pair of horses that I could use during the winter. I would do visitations to Edmore, which was about 40 miles northwest of Goodeve, near Foam Lake. But Ituna was the centre of a powerful Ukrainian Greek Catholic community with full pastoral facilities, a monastery, an orphanage, and sisters to teach in their schools. This made it more difficult for our Orthodox parish to expand as rapidly as in other areas.

Dmytro Kitsul, who farmed 16 miles north of Ituna, had purchased building materials to build a new home for his family. But a group of our faithful implored Kitsul to leave his materials in Ituna and build the new Orthodox church in Ituna. Lev Batrakalo, a carpenter, who had arrived from Eastern Ukraine, also agreed to help.

The church was not yet fully built when the parishioners wanted to have a Divine Liturgy served. A typically cold Saskatchewan winter forced them to install a camp stove to heat the church. The chimney had not yet been installed, so they removed a window pane to allow the smoke to exit. Unfortunately, the window they chose was on the windward side and the church soon filled with smoke. It was so cold that the water flask on the altar froze. I had to wear my vestments on top of my fur coat, in order to be able to serve the Divine Liturgy.

After the Feast of Jordan, as is our custom, the priest visits the home of each parishioner to bless it with Holy Water and to meet, chat, and become acquainted with all the members of the family. I always kept a careful record of each name and visit. The secretary of the Church Council, Mykola Boykowich, accompanied me to document the families. We even stopped at the home of Mr. Tkach, a Greek Catholic, who invited us in for lunch. His brother Fedir attended our Orthodox church regularly. Tkach told us, "We are all brethren of the one God," and after lunch gave us a generous donation for our new church.

We worked hard, raising money for the new church to furnish it properly with icons and church vestments. Many years later, when I was in Toronto, the people of Ituna sent me a letter of thanks, and included a postal money order as a gift of love in appreciation of the work I had helped them with. From the very beginning of my missionary work, I have always felt blessed that I was surrounded by generous and loving parishioners. All I had to do was show them Christian love and to teach them to tithe. This would bind them as an integral part of one church family. Whenever I asked for help, they would never refuse me.

Once, in an emergency, I was called to Goodeve. I left my horses at Shymko's livery stable and rushed off to the station. I desperately searched all my pockets and found out I had no money. A kindly man at the wicket paid for my ticket, and as the train had begun to move, I rushed to get on board, and didn't even have an opportunity to get the name of my benefactor to thank him.

My third son, Orest, was born in Goodeve, in June, 1928. Zenon, my eldest, had already started school. I had been elected chairman of the School Trustees and whenever the need arose, I substituted as a teacher. We enjoyed two great years in this district.

My friend, Peter Lazarowich, who was then the rector of the Michael Hrushevsky Institute (now St. John's Institute), sent me a letter begging me to come and rescue St. John's parish in Edmonton. A couple of years earlier, the parish had purchased a church on 96th Street (the church with the sloping floor) with monies borrowed from an elderly member, John Melnyk. This church was to serve Edmonton and the surrounding areas. There was a desperate need for Church Services, but the church remained closed because there was no priest to serve them. Edmonton, the capital of Alberta, had a strong base of Ukrainian intelligentsia, businessmen, manufacturers, professionals, doctors, lawyers etc. Peter warned me that it would be a tough challenge for me. I had some reservations about my own shortcomings, but I would never allow myself to back down from a challenge.

We quickly sold almost everything we had accumulated so carefully, much of it at less than half of what we had paid, and on November 1, 1928, my family and I set out for Edmonton. We were now a family of five, my wife, Katherine, at age 25, Zenon six years old, William at two, and Orest at five months.

BOOK 7

ALBERTA

*My mission is to help them believe
they can become the people
God wants them to be,
and as God's children,
do the things that mean something.*

Fr. Peter Sametz

My Edmonton Era

Our trip to Edmonton proved to be eventful. Along the way from Goodeve, we stopped in Cudworth, where my wife's elderly parents were living. We decided that my wife and three sons would stay there for a short visit, while I would continue on to Edmonton and properly prepare for their arrival.

I went on to Saskatoon where I spent the night at St. Petro Mohyla Institute. In the morning I changed the oil in the car, gassed up, and drove on through Lloydminster to Vegreville. My dear friend Peter Svarich (a founding member of our Church) noticed that my car needed oil and topped it off. As I drove on a few miles further, the motor seized up. The car was towed to a garage in Chipman, completely useless. Apparently, when the oil was changed in Saskatoon, the drain port was not properly secured, causing a gradual loss of oil. The engine overheated, the wiring had melted and the motor seized up.

I took the train to Edmonton where I slept over at the Michael Hrushevsky Institute (now St. John's Institute). In the morning, I went to the Essex car dealer who sold me a new car (with borrowed money). I returned to Chipman and transferred the pillows, quilts, and the baggage I had left in my old car. I received a credit of $600 for the body of the old car, which was like brand new.

At my first meeting with the Edmonton parish, the president started by complaining about our church leadership, and why the Church had accepted Fr. Halicky into the ranks of our clergy. Fr. Philip Halicky was a talented priest, a former rector of the Hrushevsky Institute there, but when he suddenly left them, it had been a big blow to the community there. I felt I had to diffuse this negativity immediately and so I explained to the parish how in the past decade our Church became successful and was able to grow when it accepted well-educated Ukrainian-Canadian candidates, like Fr. Halicky. I pointed out that Edmonton as yet had not even bothered to send delegates to any of the Church Sobors (conferences). Even when we welcomed Archbishop Ioan (Teodorovich) as our Primate, they were not present. The need was great, but with such a shortage of clergy in the Church, there was no room for complaining. They admitted they had not participated, and this effectively diffused the confrontational atmosphere of the meeting.

The Edmonton parish was particularly blessed with a very active, bright and gifted Women's Association at the church. It organized the church choir, the Sunday Schools and the Ukrainian language schools and made sure that all events at the church hummed with activity. Wherever I served, the truly successful parishes were those where the women of the parish were most active. They were the ones working for the development of education, language, his-

Divine Liturgy, welcoming Archbishop Ioan (Teodorovich).
St. Michael's Church, Winnipeg, Manitoba, 1924.
Fr. Sametz, Fr. Sawchuk, Archbishop Ioan and Fr. Stratychuk.

tory and culture, as well as organizing our Sunday
Schools. Truly, they set the highest standards for all the
social and cultural activities in a parish, and were its soul
and conscience. We often say that of the four corners of
the church at least three are supported by the women.

Peter Lazarowich had told the parish that I had been
a teacher in the Saskatoon area and that during our national conventions I had prepared and directed plays and

The original St. John's Church, Edmonton, Alberta.

Ukrainian school at St. John's Church, Edmonton, 1929.
Fr. Sametz is standing on the left.

concerts. The stage at the Hrushevsky Institute was commandeered as the parishioners decided to produce the musical *Natalka Poltavka*, a gem of Ukrainian literature and musical drama. The local Ukrainian Veterans Association had many gifted members who joined in the production, and the Women's Association also volunteered its talents. The veteran organization was at the Ukrainian National Union Hall, which was located in a brick factory outside the city limits. I had to pick them up by car and bring them to the rehearsals at the Institute.

Mr. Zavadiuk, a long-time teacher at the Institute and choir conductor at the church, as well as teacher of music, agreed to help us. The problem was that he lived in Carvel, about 30 miles west of the city, so I had to drive him back and forth for each rehearsal. Zavadiuk knew where to find the musical talent—at the Institute and at the church. He even managed to pull together a small orchestra for the production.

Our parish *diak* (cantor), Stephan Zdril, a gifted baritone, played the role of Makohonenko (the village elder), while Mrs. Emily Proniuk played Natalka. The production was a great success and the audience loved it. The proceeds of the production helped salvage our poor impoverished parish on 96th Street. St. John's Church later attained the status of a cathedral, and from its humble beginnings, there grew four more Ukrainian Orthodox parishes in Edmonton.

Church affairs were always complicated, but we now had the emergence of a new Ukrainian identity replacing the old regional divisions of Volyniak, Galician, Hutsul, etc. Along with this newfound identity we had the historic return to *the Faith of our forefathers.* The new emphasis on education and literacy was *opening the door* to careers in the professions, skilled vocations and the world of politics. Most important was the realization that we now had a golden opportunity to be *as good as or even better* than others. Canadian society gave us freedom of religion, freedom of expression, and freedom of choice. We also had our new motto—*Self-reliance, Self-help, Self-respect, and Self-worth!*

Edmonton, like Winnipeg, was the centre of Ukrainian immigration in Alberta. Nearly every fifth or sixth person in Edmonton was of Ukrainian descent, and the proportions remain the same, even today. Membership in our Institutes was open to Orthodox students and those of other affiliations. The rector, Peter Lazarowich, was a tall young dynamo, an accomplished choir conductor and a musician, who started to develop an interest in church matters and, by example, raised the bar for participation as a church family. Before I came to Edmonton, Fr. P. Bilon, a former chaplain in the Ukrainian Air Force, followed by Fr. D. Seneta, who was a former Greek Catholic priest, tried to establish some sort of church presence, but both soon departed for greener pastures in the United

States. It was left up to me to try and set a firm foundation for the church and the Institute.

I lectured the young students at the Institute on the Ukrainian language, culture, traditions, history, and on our Faith. I registered at the University of Alberta to further my own education, but the demands of my missionary work for the Church and our community in Edmonton did not leave me any time to pursue this opportunity. For me, it was *the school of life* which provided me with a very effective learning curve.

The massive second wave of Ukrainian immigrants, which came after World War I to the outlying communities of Alberta, settled west towards Wildwood and Seba Beach, north towards Westlock, and northwest as far as Grande Prairie. On Sundays I would serve the Divine Liturgy at St. John's Church on 96th Street, and then during the week I would go out to the outlying areas to perform Church Services. The newcomers were mainly from Volyn, and although they were previously served by the Russian Bishop Arseny (Chakhovtsev), these Volyniaks accepted me more readily. On one of my visits, accompanied by my cantor, Stephan Zdril, a heavy rain caused us to slide off the partially gravelled Jasper Highway. We had to walk to the nearest village where we found a drayman (a tow man with horses) who came to haul my car out of the ditch. Needless to say, our trip proved to be more eventful than planned.

I also established excellent relations with other Faiths and Churches in Edmonton. I felt it was important to set our place among them and to affirm our presence in the larger Edmonton religious community. Once, Anglican Bishop Henry Allen Gray even invited me to accompany him to the Anglican Synod that was to be held in Canterbury, England. At that time I could not leave my extended parishes, but I strongly felt that we must pray together, and have dialogue with all our Christian brethren to improve our image and relations in Canada.

Our debates on the Gospels with Bishop Gray were among the highlights of our relationship. Our approach to the interpretation of readings from the Gospels was quite different. He gave me many books of famous sermons by Anglican and Catholic priests, who had interpreted the Gospels literally, as a history. Respectfully, I had to differ, because I strongly felt that my role as a priest was to interpret the Gospels and their Truths in terms that my faithful could relate to in the hardships of their everyday life. How could I relate to the bishop the feelings of the *misteria* (mystery) of Ukrainian Orthodoxy, the *misteria* that was built up over centuries of tears—tears of sorrow, tears of joy, and tears of thanksgiving. How could I explain *the feel* of the Faith of our forefathers? How could I tell the bishop, that if Jesus came among us, where two or more gather, it would not be because of the pomp and circumstance of religion? All He taught us was to love each other, and that this would save us from the depths of despair, and give us hope and joy, and a future to look forward to. Just quoting words, without relating them to each and every one of us on a personal basis, was not what was needed.

My training as a teacher taught me that I had to communicate the message and teachings of the Lord in words that my parishioners would understand, and to make the teachings more relevant in their daily lives. My role was to reaffirm the message of hope and love that would sustain them during their long and difficult periods of isolation, troubles, illnesses, deaths and despair, which they were experiencing on a daily basis. The strength they needed was in their Faith, and in their understanding that they were not alone. As a teacher and a priest, my role was to serve their needs, and to help them dream of a glorious future, if not for them, then for the lives of their children. Theirs was to be the Glory in the Afterlife.

Although I never had the luxury of delving deeply into the *misteria* of our Orthodox Faith, I always felt and lived it. Every day I had to give meaning and relevance to the teachings of the Gospels, and I believed that this path was right for our people. To me Bishop Gray was always a true friend, and I think that deep down inside he may have agreed with me. My sermons would always revolve around the one True Commandment of the Lord—to love God and to love thy brother.

On May 2, 1930, we were blessed with the birth of our youngest child, our first and only daughter, Olga. She was the first child born to us in a hospital, the Royal Alexandra Hospital, with Dr. John Verchomin attending. In spite of his extremely busy medical practice, Dr. Verchomin and his family were one of the most active members of our parish, and true founders and supporters of our Church.

I always had the strong old-country attachment to the land, and knew that when I owned my own property, we could always survive. All it took was a cow or two, a few chickens, a garden of our own, mother's exceptional farm management skills, and her love of looking after the bees for sweet honey. Together with Mr. Yanishewsky, a talented carpenter and church builder, we purchased adjacent properties, about 14 acres each, three miles west of Jasper Place, then on the western boundaries of Edmonton. Mother put in four acres of clover for her bees, feed for the cow, planted another acre of strawberries and put in a huge garden. A small barn was built for the cow. For us, Mr. Yanishewsky built a small cottage, complete with a little veranda and *outside facilities*. Mr. Yanishewsky also built a house for his family on the neighbouring property, but because he was always off building churches for our new communities in Alberta and Saskatchewan, his family chose to live in the city and they soon sold their parcel of land to a Mr. Fred Wilson.

The Sametz family in Jasper Place, Alberta, 1932. Standing left to right: Zenon and Katherine Sametz; sitting left to right: Orest, Fr. Peter Sametz and William; in front: Olga.

Archbishop Ioan (Teodorovich) and Sporty, Jasper Place.

Mr. Wilson was an old bachelor and a fur trapper north of Athabasca during the winter, partnering with his Ukrainian friend. One day, while working the trap lines, Fred discovered his partner face down, frozen to death with his arms outstretched. Fred came down south to get me to bury his friend in the north country they both loved so much. While I was packing to leave, Fred stood over the only furnace grill that was located in the middle of the house over the partially excavated basement. Trappers would wear two pairs of *long johns* (long winter underwear) which they removed, about once a year, when they readied themselves for their annual bath. Fred had lived with his Ukrainian friend, who taught him the magic curing power of raw garlic, not only eaten, but also worn around the neck and under the *long johns* to ward off all illnesses and evil omens. The combined attar of old garlic and about nine months of accumulated sweat absolutely flooded the house. Mother tried to manoeuvre Fred away from the hot air register by offering him a cup of hot tea. Fred just thanked her and said that he was just enjoying the warmth. After Fred and I left for Athabasca, mother dressed the children in their winter clothing and opened the doors to let in the outside air to freshen the house, at minus 20 degrees Fahrenheit.

After Fred and I came to where his trap lines were located, the body of his friend was removed from the wood shed, still in its frozen state. It was decided to bury him *as is*. How they folded his frozen arms to fit into the homemade coffin Fred had made, I never asked or wanted to know. Fred generously converted a cold cellar that he had previously dug in the permafrost into a grave, which I consecrated.

With the rapid assimilation and adoption of Canadian lifestyles by my talented and success-driven parishioners, I anticipated that Edmonton would be chosen as the *cathedra* (official seat) of the Bishop of the Western Eparchy. As early as 1933, it appeared probable and preferable that the administration of our Church in Canada be moved to Edmonton from Winnipeg. I resigned my position in favour of Fr. Sawchuk who had assumed the office of administrator of the Church in Winnipeg. I asked for a new charge, and chose to move back to Saskatchewan, to where I was eventually reassigned. This was one of the biggest mistakes of my life.

Four months later, I received a letter from the Consistory stating that Fr. Sawchuk would not be leaving Winnipeg, and that Fr. Eronim Hrycyna would be coming to Edmonton to replace him.

It was 1933, and the Depression hit Saskatchewan much harder than Alberta. Farmers were only getting 25¢ a bushel for wheat, and the parishes could hardly get $10 together for a Sunday Service. I was sorry to leave Edmonton and the fine people I had worked with. I should never have left them after all the missionary work that had been done. I assured the parishioners that Fr. Hrycyna was a good priest, but they felt that I was abandoning them, and I think that I let myself down even more. No one ever said a word about it, but I don't think that the Edmonton parish ever forgave me for this move.

I left my family on our fourteen-acre lot, while I went ahead to Saskatchewan to try and make some sort of arrangements to move them there. It took me until October, 1934, almost two years, before I had enough money to move the family and find a home to rent in Wakaw, the centre of my new parishes.

Originally, we started school at Jasper Place, Alberta, which was about a three-mile walk each way. Whenever it turned brutally cold, there were days that attendance was impossible. The following year we were transferred to Winterbourne School in Stony Plain. Here we were provided with lessons that have lasted us a lifetime. The students from grade 1 to grade 8 were an interesting mix. The children were of Scottish, Irish and French-Canadian farmers, plus the "half-breed" Métis from the Indian Reservation. The government provided schools for the Indian children on the Reservation, but children from "mixed" marriages had to go outside the Reservation to our school. They rode to school bareback on their ponies, and were amazing horsemen. I often thought that they were like Ukrainian Cossacks. I re-

member one of them, an overgrown sixteen-year-old in my grade 4 class, showing off his amazing abilities in front of a group of admiring girls he was trying to impress. He rode full gallop around the school standing on the rear haunches of his pony. When the pony stumbled, he flipped off and broke his arm. No one dared to laugh.

Our teacher, Miss Bataille, a four-foot-six "giant", of necessity ruled with an iron fist. She took me aside one day and said, "William, you and your brother Zenon are the only ones who have read every book in our tiny library, including the Books of Knowledge. For sure, you were not born with a silver spoon in your mouth. For you the ladder of success in your life starts right here in the middle of this classroom. All you have to do is to get on that ladder and climb, rung by rung, until you climb right through the roof. It is your choice to make." I will never forget Miss Bataille and the great motivating influence she had on my life.

BOOK 8

SASKATCHEWAN
THE GREAT DEPRESSION
BACK TO ALBERTA

*He told us to dream the impossible,
to attempt and create the impossible,
and that He will always be with us
to guide us to our everlasting life.*

Fr. Peter Sametz

Wakaw, Saskatchewan

I always felt close to the people who settled in the area of Wakaw and St. Julien, where I had taught earlier. The parishioners built a National Home (community centre) beside the church. The area teachers gathered there with me to put on theatrical presentations, concerts, lectures and readings for the people. Although most of the locals could not read or write, many of the older people would memorize every reading we presented. It always amazed me how they could harness the power of their memory to compensate for this lack of literacy.

My in-laws, the Bambuchs, lived in Cudworth. They had immigrated from Horodenka in the 1890s with the Kotelko, Hawrysh, and Nykyforuk families, who had arrived as *Austriaky* (with Austrian passports). I wanted my children to get to know their grandparents, and to acquaint them with the area where I first taught school in Canada.

It would be a huge understatement to say that the Wakaw area was an *interesting* Ukrainian centre. Many of the Ukrainians who settled there came from the same areas and villages of the old country. They brought with them their own hillbilly battles, not unlike those of *the Hatfields and the McCoys*. These centuries-old family feuds, well developed and well honed, were transferred to this new venue, and the feuds were restarted with great enthusiasm and fervour.

It was here in Wakaw that a young John Diefenbaker first set up his law practice with my countryman, Michael Stechishin, as his partner. I became close friends with John and we spent many a coffee hour in deep and serious discussions about the future of the new Canada, its potential, and our place in this new spectrum. Diefenbaker had many opportunities to hone his courtroom skills among the denizens of Wakaw, who provided him with many interesting and varied cases of conflicts that they created among themselves.

These Wakaw feuds were the cause of much sorrow and worry to me. There were many times when I would be called upon to perform Church Services or provide Holy Sacraments for one family, while the *other side* (and often there were quite a few sides) would threaten me, even physically. The feuds tested my peacekeeping abilities. Fortunately, there was never an occasion when I was in any way physically harmed.

The midnight burning of the Alvena Lumber Yard, and the subsequent shootout, reputed to be the work of one of the family gangs, was never actually solved, certainly because fear of reprisal was a factor.

Until my family arrived, I lived with a retired couple, the Hulianatys. Mr. Hulianaty was a retired carpenter and a fulltime fisherman at Wakaw Lake. They were a wonderfully hospitable couple who dried the fish in their home. The home was spotlessly clean, but the heavy attar of drying fish always permeated the whole house.

As a carpenter, Mr. Hulianaty was also the local coffin maker. When we arrived in Wakaw, we rented the house next door. We knew that Mr. Hulianaty would often take his afternoon naps in a special coffin he had made for himself, which he kept in the garage at the back of the house. We would often sneak around the corner to watch him take full advantage of the comfort of that coffin, well in advance of its ultimate purpose. As long as he lay there snoring away, we were reassured that he had not yet passed on to his just reward.

Mr. Bettner, the town constable, was very careful not to get mixed up with the various feuds around him. He justified his lofty position by effectively enforcing the 9 p.m. town curfew for all children under 16 years of age. My older brother Zenon was often engaged in a foot race with the constable between our house and Kvasnytsia's General Store, in order to get an urgent message to my father.

The General Store was the town's central meeting place. My father often used this venue to meet and chat with his parishioners. I am sure this was his way of doing missionary work, and it was an effective method of communication. He used to keep in close contact with

each family and to encourage them to come and partici-
pate in the Church Services. This "one-on-one contact"
was his way to get each and every one to feel important
and "in on things." It always worked well for father.

Although I was only in grade 4, this was the fourth
public school I had attended. There were McCauley and
Jasper Place Public Schools in Edmonton, then Winter-
bourne in Stony Plain, and now Wakaw in Saskatche-
wan. By grade 8 I had added St. Julien's Kolomyia
School, Winterbourne, again, and then Ryerson in To-
ronto. Seven different schools in eight junior grades was
not conducive to establishing any long-term childhood
friendships. We met a lot of wonderful people along the
way, but there was no time for bonding or networking.

St. Julien

The Great Depression of the thirties hit Saskatchewan with a resounding wallop. Furthermore, the farmers
were dealt rust blights, drought and a vicious grasshopper
plague. A black cloud of grasshoppers would descend on a
field of grain and wipe it out in less than 20 minutes.
When the grasshoppers landed on the train tracks at Wakaw, the trains had problems getting any traction on the
greasy tracks the grasshoppers would leave behind.

We could not afford to continue renting and sustain-
ing ourselves in Wakaw. The following July, the parish in

*Ceremonial welcome of Archbishop Ioan (Teodorovich).
St. Julien, Saskatchewan, 1936.*

Hahilky (spring dances), Easter Monday, St. Julien.

The parish "manse" in St. Julien, Saskatchewan.

The Kolomyia School in St. Julien, Saskatchewan.

St. Julien arranged for us to stay on a piece of land, close to the church, where there was an abandoned two-room house. Here, at least we could grow our own food for self-subsistence.

Although it was difficult for everyone, in retrospect it appears that no one can start lower on the economic ladder than a preacher's kid that comes from Saskatchewan in the Dirty Thirties.

St. Julien was located in the middle of my circle of parishes, which extended from Vonda and Meacham to the south, then north to Smuts, Cudworth, Alvena, Carpenter, Wakaw and St. Julien. The parishes extended further north to Prince Albert, east to Tway and Yellow Creek, and then west to Rosthern, Krydor, Hafford and Richard.

I taught my two sons, Zenon and William, to sing the Vespers, the Matins and the responses of the Divine Liturgy. I would take one of them with me whenever I knew there was no local cantor to help the parishioners sing the responses. I taught them both to drive a car at the tender age of 12, in order to relieve me on long and arduous trips between the parishes, and to take me to railway stations.

There were times when the parish had no money to pay the priest after a Church Service, but the good people were always willing to share what little they had. I remember one Sunday after a Service in Smuts (now a ghost town), the parishioners gave us a live rooster. It was given to us live because, before the age of refrigeration, this was the only way to transport a future meal fresh. My *new* car was a used Chevrolet that I had purchased from the Sagy brothers in Meacham. I designated William, who was in the back seat, as the official custodian of the rooster. This was the rooster's first introduction to automobile travel and the experience affected its innards. We were honoured with the white residue of its stomach. When we arrived home in St. Julien, I reminded William that the rooster had been his responsibility, so the cleanup of the car was also his responsibility.

In St. Julien we attended the one-room Kolomyia School and our teacher was William Magus, who was also my father's cantor. All 40 children, from grade 1 to grade 8, were from families that belonged to our church, except one Ukrainian girl whose family belonged to the Baptist Church. At that time, our first language was Ukrainian, but Magus would not tolerate any spoken Ukrainian in the classroom or during recess. He had the first radio we had ever seen or heard. I remember the big treat he gave us all, by allowing us to listen to the "Adventures of Tarzan."

Harvest was a time of hard work and the celebration of bountiful crops. Everyone worked very hard.

Even at 10 years of age I worked the grain box together with my younger brother, Orest, who was eight at that time. The grain box was a box wagon pulled by a team of horses that was filled with the grain spout of the threshing machine. Once full, we would drive the wagon to the granary where we emptied the load with bushel-sized scoops. Pay was minimal, but as we moved from farm to farm, each farmer's wife worked hard to outdo the other wives with fabulous feasts of Ukrainian cooking.

During this period, my mother's mother, Baba Bambuch, passed away in Cudworth in 1934. And Grandfather Bambuch passed away in 1936. I remember grandfather's funeral very well. After the elders built the coffin, and prepared and dressed the body, they placed grandfather inside. Everyone gathered for the wake. While the children played, the parents exchanged reminiscences, as well as tall tales. The children would listen to these stories from the adjacent room. Some of them were quite horrific, embellished especially for our sake.

One story gave me nightmares for years to come. It was about a young boy who allegedly died and had been laid out in his coffin. As was the custom, the coffin was closed at night. In the morning, when the coffin was opened, the boy lay with his hands raised up as if pressed against the lid. Apparently, he'd had some sort of seizure and had stopped breathing. During the night he revived, but was suffocated by the closed lid of the coffin.

We began to realize that the education of our children was becoming a problem. The younger ones were still in public school here in St. Julien, but my eldest son, Zenon, was completing grade 9 through correspondence courses sent to him from Regina. We were considering sending him to St. Petro Mohyla Institute in Saskatoon.

Our parish in Hafford had just completed building a new Orthodox church, ready for consecration. Hafford had become a very active centre of Ukrainian activity, social and cultural. There was a large Ukrainian Greek Catholic church, a National Home (community centre) and now a new Orthodox church. After the blessing of the cross, which was to be placed atop the central dome, we watched with bated breath as our contractor strapped it across his back, climbed up the ladder to the roof and then inched his way up by rope to the very top of the dome. It was a remarkable sight to watch him set the cross atop the new church.

In 1937, I received a letter from Fr. Sawchuk in Winnipeg stating that the Church had new priests ready to take my place in Saskatchewan among my well-established parishes. I was being reassigned to Alberta, to serve the new parishes that were being organized. I was happy that we could return to our house and our 14 acres outside Edmonton. High school and university education would be available for my children. But it was 1937 and the economy was still in the throes of the Depression.

Parishes served by Fr. Peter Sametz.
Photos taken from his "Open Scrapbook."

167

Parishes served by Fr. Peter Sametz.
Photos taken from his "Open Scrapbook."

Our people survived the Depression because of their ability to become self-sufficient despite the Depression, the drought, the wheat rust or the grasshopper plagues. Life could only get better for them. Each year they seemed to manage to make something out of nothing, and slowly progressed upward. They did not start by losing everything because they had nothing to lose to start with. Every year was like a step up the ladder.

Back to Alberta

At the Sixteenth Sobor of our Church, Fr. Kernitsky described my new parish as the whole of Northern Alberta. This included Lac La Biche, Bruderheim, Redwater, Radway, Fedorah, Boyle, Smoky Lake and Vilna. My parish also included Stony Plain, Seba Beach and Wildwood in the west, and Calmar and Thorsby in the south. Later, my missionary district was extended to include Calgary, as well as Vernon and Vancouver in British Columbia. Often I would be gone for a month or longer.

Mother and the children sustained and supported themselves with the garden and livestock, which included a couple of cows and a calf that always managed to get out. No fence could hold her, even when we equipped her with a yoke around her neck. Mother lovingly tended up to 19 beehives as well. After every rain, the children would head out to a drainage ditch, at the south end of our property, to pick a pail or two of mushrooms to add to their daily diet. In the adjacent woods they would find golden-topped *kozari* (birch boletes—mushrooms).

My father's extended absences while on his mission-ary trail were especially hard on mother. There was never any money, and she had to raise four small chil-dren on her own. She had no one to talk to, and it was not surprising that she would often become despondent and depressed. Every evening, after a hard day's work, she would just go to bed, while we would continue to read our library books by the coal oil lamp, which was our only source of light.

When the Province decided to regrade and resurface the Jasper Highway, the contractor rented two acres of mother's clover patch for a tent camp where the work gang could sleep and eat. I was hired to clean the kitchen garbage. The chef would always kindly "gift wrap" left-over meats and sausages and place them in the trash can for me to pick up.

I remember one memorable trip that I took with my father, about 100 miles northeast of Edmonton, with Mr. Svityk, an active community stalwart from Calgary. We swung off a passable road, onto a trail, between smoking stumps, on lands freshly broken by homesteaders of this area. The smoke hung in the air like a heavy morning fog. We reached a large clearing, where we saw a tall

Parishes served by Fr. Peter Sametz.
Photos taken from his "Open Scrapbook."

Parishes served by Fr. Peter Sametz.
Photos taken from his "Open Scrapbook."

Orthodox birch cross and a birch altar. The perimeter of the clearing was surrounded with wagons filled with families who had not seen a priest since they had arrived in the area, about 16 to 18 years earlier.

After the Divine Liturgy, my father performed the Holy Sacrament of Baptism on 126 children who were gathered in a circle around the altar. They ranged in age from three days old, to 17 years, some almost twice my size and age. The depth of faith of these pioneers, that I felt that day as an 11-year-old, was a gift that will always be with me.

On to Vancouver

My new mission extended almost 900 miles east to west, and about 300 miles north to south. The faithful were building their churches in various areas at an accelerated rate, and required regular Church Services. I advised Fr. Sawchuk and the Consistory to prepare at least three more priests to come to these areas, to serve these parishes properly.

In August, 1938, I set out by car on a trip to Vancouver. With me was my eldest son, Zenon, as well as the owner of the Ukrainian Book and Music Store in Edmonton, Dmytro Ferbey, and a young lawyer, Dmytro Yanda, with his talented wife. Along the way we stopped to visit the various parishes we passed by on our trip to Calgary.

We crossed the American border at Waterton Lakes National Park, then travelled through the glorious Rocky Mountains. We enjoyed vistas that only God could create. We stopped in Seattle where we saw the Pacific Ocean for the first time in our lives. In the morning, as we headed north, we encountered fog so thick and heavy that it was impossible to see. Zenon led us by walking ahead of the car to make sure that we stayed on the road, until the fog eventually lifted.

There was no church in Vancouver, so I served the Divine Liturgy at the National Home. The people were delighted to receive me and my distinguished co-travellers. I was invited to move my family to Vancouver. They offered my family and me a parish home and the princely sum of $150 per month, and they promised that they would build a church immediately. I was totally over-whelmed.

On our return trip, we took the Canadian route back through Vernon where I served the Divine Liturgy in the National Home. After the Service, the people held a din-ner, at which Ferbey, Yanda and his wife, spoke to an en-raptured audience. We continued on through Banff to Calgary, and then we proceeded north towards Edmon-ton. We were flagged down by John Svityk, who was then a manager with the Western Life Insurance Company. He told me that there was an urgent telegram from Toronto, Ontario, waiting for me in Edmonton.

When we arrived in Edmonton, we stopped at the law office of Peter Lazarowich to read the telegram that had arrived from Theodore Humeniuk, the president of the Toronto parish, who was Peter's brother-in-law. There was also a letter from Fr. Sawchuk requesting that I immediately move to Toronto to save the parish.

The St. Vladimir (now St. Volodymyr) parish had been established in Toronto in 1926. It owned a vacant lot at 400 Bathurst Street, but with borrowed money had purchased an old building, the Odd Fellows Hall, beside it at 404 Bathurst Street for $18,500. With a combined debt load of $23,000, the parish had dwindled to 22 active family members. The rest, alarmed by this heavy financial burden, had scattered and their priest abandoned them, leaving for America.

At this time, life was beginning to go very well for me and my family. We had our own home on 14 acres, three miles west of Jasper Place, then the western boundary of Edmonton. We had a cow that produced fresh milk, and we had honey to sweeten our life. Zenon had just won an essay contest sponsored by the *Edmonton Journal*. The title of his essay was *A Prediction of World War II*, after Hitler invaded Austria.

Zenon was in grade 12 at Victoria High School and every day he pedalled eight miles each way on the bicycle he purchased with the money he had won for his essay. I think that Zenon's motivation for writing the essay was the bicycle, which saved him the three-mile walk to the bus, which would then take him another five miles to school. Coincidentally, Zenon's mathematics teacher was Mr. Shortcliffe, who had taught me at Wesley College in Winnipeg back in 1914.

I had just returned from Vancouver with a great offer. Instead, I was going to Toronto. I have often thought of the injustice of this to my wife and family. They had helped me acquire a nice home and a fine property near Edmonton. Also, I was leaving behind the wonderful parishes in Alberta, which were now well-established. The Consistory had to supply three priests to take my place, to provide the parishes with regular Church Services.

In 1938, during an economically depressed time, we sold our home, our farm, and our car, at rock bottom bargain prices. We bundled our meagre belongings—mostly clothes, my books and my newspaper files of the *Ukrainian Voice* and our Church journal, *Visnyk* (The Herald), which I had saved from its inception. We took our pillows and quilts and away we went by train to Toronto.

My friend from Vita, Kulachkowsky, often said to me, "You are a very good priest, but in personal financial matters, you are very close to being quite stupid!" I agreed with him, but I always felt that the Good Lord would provide, and He eventually did.

BOOK 9

THE TORONTO SAGA
1938-1949

He is ...my refuge and my fortress,
my God, in whom I trust.

Psalm 91

What is the problem?
Why is it a problem?
What do we do about it?

We can't solve it with the same mindset that created it.

Fr. Peter Sametz

Our Arrival in Toronto

It was a very long journey for us in September, 1938. We travelled coach class for four days and four nights, through three time zones, arriving in Toronto bone-weary and hungry. We met a Michael Evanytsky on the train. He had worked as section hand on the railway for over five years in order to earn enough money to bring his wife, daughter Katrusia, and young son Walter to Canada. They were waiting for him in Toronto.

We were met by a welcoming committee of one, Michael Materyn, who was the church cantor. He was the father of Myroslava, who later became the wife of John Yaremko Q.C., the first Ukrainian Cabinet Minister in the Province of Ontario. Mr. Materyn drove us to our *new* home, a rented house at 2 Roseberry Avenue, which was beside the original Toronto Western Hospital and across the street from the church. This house was so poorly insulated that during the first winter the bed covers on the children's beds were covered with snow that blew in through the window frames. Thank goodness we had brought our warm down quilts with us from out west.

Instead of the generous offer from the Vancouver parish, I was paid only $90 a month (the original promise was $100 a month) in Toronto. But I never saw my pay check for over a year. The house we lived in belonged to the parish president, Theodore Humeniuk, who made sure that the monthly rent of $29 was paid first. We were left with the balance of $61 to pay for food, clothing, telephone, power, water and coal for the furnace. I had paid for our move to Toronto out of the meagre money we had left over from the sale of our Edmonton home and car. We were flat broke.

This was one of the darkest moments of our lives. We held a family meeting at which I cried and regretted the injustice I had unloaded on them. But my family rallied behind me. Mother, with her sewing skills, went to work at the Tip Top Tailors clothing factory as a seamstress. She managed to earn $8 a week for five ten-hour weekdays plus a Saturday shift from 8 a.m. to 2 p.m. There was no money for Zenon to pursue his higher education. Zenon entered grade 12 at Harbord Collegiate Institute, but in two weeks he was transferred to grade 13, and was finishing high school during our first year in Toronto.

William, in grade 8 at Ryerson Public School, went to sell newspapers—*The Globe and Mail*, *Toronto Daily Star* and *Toronto Telegram*. The newspapers sold for 3¢ each and he would earn 9¢ for every 10 newspapers that he sold. William shared the newsstand with William Malayko, the famous *newsie* who would save his pennies all year in order to go to the Metropolitan Opera in New York City, completely outfitted in top hat and tails. Malayko was a partial invalid and soon turned over his newsstands to William, after he had proven himself. The newsstands were located at the eastern entrance of Union Station, serving the morning train commuters, and later in the day, at the entrance to the Toronto Stock Exchange on Bay Street, as well as the entrance to the original Bank of Toronto at the corner of King and Bay Streets. Rushing between work and school on roller skates, William, with his newspapers, would often earn more than mother and I combined. This is how we managed to survive and pay for Zenon's university education.

Zenon entered the University of Toronto at age 16. His application for medicine was turned down because he was under the accepted age of 18. He took sociology and political science instead. When he graduated at 21 he became an associate lecturer, while working on his master's degree.

I thought of my predecessors who had served the St. Vladimir (now St. Volodymyr) Toronto parish before me. They were exceptionally talented priests. Fr. Petro Bilon, the priest who served the first Divine Liturgy in Toronto in 1926, was the famous chaplain of the Ukrainian Air Force, a learned orator, with a great voice. He had preceded me at the Edmonton parish. The next priest was Fr. Dmytro Leschyshyn, also very talented. The third was Fr. Philip Halicky, a former teacher from Bukovyna and a rector of the Michael Hrushevsky Institute (now St. John's Institute) in Edmonton. How could I compare my talents with these gifted priests who had given up on the Toronto parish?

I really had no choice. I could not afford to return to my familiar parishes in Manitoba, Saskatchewan or Alberta. My life savings were all gone. I delved deeply into my soul and felt that the Good Lord had given me the gift of love—love for my people, love for our choral liturgical music, and the deep love and profound respect for my parents and my family. This love was the source of my strength to sustain me through these darker moments of my missionary work.

During our first three years in Toronto, just living was a difficult hand-to-mouth existence. If mother, Orest and William had not been working to support the family and pay for Zenon's and their own schooling, we would have never made it.

The Start

On October 23, 1938, I celebrated my first Divine Liturgy in the Green Room on the second floor of 404 Bathurst, which was converted weekly, on Sunday mornings, into a church. The faithful packed the room to overflowing, wanting to have a look and size up the *new* priest. The Matins were sung by Michael Materyn and the choir conductor, Michael Levak, who had gathered a small choir to sing the responses of the Divine Liturgy.

After the Service, our church elder, Ilko Mandzey said to me, "Father, there were many people in church today, some who only came out of curiosity to look you over. The collection plate is great. I collected $7 and the sisterhood collected $3 for a total of $10."

Did I spend $1,000 on the move to Toronto from Edmonton only to serve in one of the poorest parishes I ever had? Even the Sunday School collections in Edmonton by twelve-year-olds, Lesia Ferbey and Natalka Michaelishen, were never less than $15. It immediately struck me that the gift of tithing was a lesson my new parishioners had to learn.

Tithing has always been an integral part of our Holy Orthodox Church. In Kyiv—the capital of Ukraine, the *City of Churches*—there once stood the Church of the Desiatyna (one-tenth, or tithes). It taught our people the gift of tithing—a percentage of one's earnings and estate that goes to the House of God. The power of tithing was feared by the godless Communists, so the Church of Tithes was the first church to be destroyed by the Bolsheviks in their attempt to break the Faith of our people.

The church elders of the Toronto parish were predominately hardworking blue-collar workers eking out an existence for themselves and their families. Out west, our farming communities were at least 20 to 40 years ahead in stability and growth. I felt that our future was in the hands of the youth and children. They were the ones that would provide the impetus and drive for the start of the biggest and wealthiest cathedral parish in Canada.

Work Begins at the Beginning

In 1938, wc founded the Ukrainian Orthodox Brotherhood of St. Volodymyr. After World War II, with people of exceptional wisdom and talent, the Brotherhood set the bar high for faith, religion and education among our faithful. I can only mention a few who contributed to the greatness of the Brotherhood. They were Professors Ivan Vlasovsky, Vasyl Ivanys, Oleksander Voronyn, Stepan Kylymnyk, Anatol Kotovych, Yaroslav Pasternak, Mykhailo Mukha, Fylymon Kulchynsky, Arsen Shumovsky, Theodore Khokhitva, and many more. Their contributions have become legendary.

I felt that proper planning was paramount to harness and direct the drive for our success. Theodore Humeniuk wrote that, "Our success stemmed from the strength of our wives—not only those who actively participated, but also those who patiently waited for their husbands to return home late from endless meetings, and who did not lock the doors before them."

During our first year, in 1939, with my background in music and theatre, we organized the young people to put on 13 concerts and 23 plays, as ways to teach our people about their heritage, history, culture, and how great a nation it was they had come from. Each event was jammed with people hungry for knowledge and entertainment. The participants of these events also felt the pride of accomplishment. As they were learning themselves, they were passing on our great traditions to others. Most importantly, these activities provided us with much needed financial support.

Our Church Services were now packed every Sunday. When the collections were to begin, I would place a bright new $2 bill as an example of paying 10% of my miserable earnings as my tithe. My church elder, Ilko Mandzey, thought his priest was completely mad, but he dutifully followed suit. It really worked. Our church collections started to double and triple.

We marshalled all the talent we could find. I knew the power that my position held as a priest. A call from the priest would bring forth an immediate response, "Yes, I will help!" even before I asked the favour. Talented people made themselves available to us. All I had to do was ask. Victor Moshuk took over from me as the director of plays and the dancing school. Then there was the famous opera singer, Mykhailo Holynsky, and the renowned choreographer, Vasyl Avramenko. Colonel Volodymyr Kedrovsky and General Volodymyr Sikevitch also contributed. When leaders led, hundreds would follow.

Regular Church Services, and the concerts, plays and various other programs we embarked upon, lifted the spirits, the pride and confidence of the parish. The Ladies Auxiliary of the Church raised almost $1,000 from various luncheons and bazaars during our first year. It was the youth, however, that provided the drive, the work, and the energy we needed. The youth of CYMK (Ukrainian Orthodox Youth of Canada) began to hold regular Sunday night dances, drawing young people like a magnet. They took over the operation of the regular weekly bingo and soon began to generate the cash flow needed for our church budget.

Initially, our bingo operation received help from Mr. Lakeman, a World War I veteran-invalid, who organized and trained us how to run a public bingo. When a police officer informed me that our bingos could not be run by an outsider or a non-member of the parish, my son William, who overheard the admonition, offered to take over as announcer and MC. My younger son, Orest, became the floor manager, and my daughter, Olga, sold the soft drinks. For three hours of work, Semen Olynyk, our treasurer, paid each of them 15¢ for their efforts. To compensate Mr. Lakeman for his loss of income at our bingo, William agreed to help him out at another church bingo. Without this bingo operation, and the work of our young people helping to run it, our parish would not have managed its huge burden of debt and survived.

The involvement of our young people, and the success they were having in saving the small parish from serious financial problems, also had another side. What happens after we pay down the debt?

My experience in Western Canada taught me that our faithful would never be satisfied with temporary facilities for our Church Services. At the meetings of our Church Executive, I began to suggest that it was time to consider the building of a church on the empty lot next to 404 Bathurst. Both Mandzey, the church elder, and I felt we were being overwhelmed with the constant assembling and disassembling of the portable *iconostasis* (altar screen of icons) and altar in the Green Room every week. We had continued to rent the room for $3-$5 an evening to the Odd Fellows for their regular weekly meetings. One of our church elders, Peter Metelsky asked, "Have you all become totally insane? There is still more than $8,000 in debt left on the mortgage, and you want to build a new church. This will put us all into bankruptcy!"

The following Easter, the Church Services were moved to the main auditorium downstairs to accommodate the huge crowd. I decided to personally go around with the collection plate. This time I put in two crisp $2 bills, and Mandzey again followed suit. While the choir sang Easter hymns, the faithful filled the collection plate to overflowing, several times. I announced to the people how proud I was of their generosity. The collection plate held over $635, truly a princely sum at that time. I thanked them sincerely, and told them that they had proven to everyone and themselves that *now we can*. But the building of the new church had to wait.

The War Years, 1939 - 1945

During this time, 404 Bathurst Street became the most famous address of our Ukrainian-Canadian community. Hundreds upon hundreds of our sons and daughters, who were in the Armed Forces, began using "404" as a drop-in centre, as part of their home away from home. Many of them never made it back from overseas.

Every Sunday, after Church Services, there were always 5 to 10 lonely soldiers that were invited to have dinner with me and my family. There were many whom I had christened, or married, or connected with in the Western parishes from which they now came. Mother could always stretch a meal to accommodate everyone.

We purchased the duplex building next to the church, with Dmytro Hunkewich and his family, and made it our home. Mother immediately rented the upper floors to university students, in order to help pay down the mortgage. At this time I was being paid $150 a month, but there were no subsidies for the manse, the telephone, the utilities or automobile.

In 1941, the Cardinal family moved to Toronto from Fort William (now Thunder Bay) and took over a Jewish funeral home on Bathurst Street, just south of our house.

Visiting soldiers of the Canadian Army with Fr. Peter Sametz, 1940.

Good Friday in Toronto, April 26, 1940.
Fr. Sametz at the Tomb of Christ with a Cossack
honour guard: William Gaba (left) and Zenon Sametz (right).

In spite of his profession, James Cardinal was one of the kindest and happiest gentlemen that I have ever known. When he took over the business, his family moved into an apartment above the funeral home. Leo, the eldest son, was away in the Air Force, Irene was at the University of Toronto and Helen, the youngest, was too young to attend school. Whenever the Cardinal family received a fresh turkey, sent from Fort William, they always shared half of it with my family. There were times when James Cardinal asked William to help at the funeral home.

Our block on Bathurst Street became a real family neighbourhood. Next door, south of the Cardinals was the Kolinko home. Mrs. Katherine Kolinko was the anchor soprano of our church choir. Her son, Jerry, always interested in the sciences, graduated from Georgia Tech. Upstairs was the home of the Prosymiak family. Hnat Prosymiak owned a garage, which kept everyone's second-hand car in operating condition. His wife, Sophie, was president of the Ladies Auxiliary (Kniahynia Olha Branch), and their daughter, Ivanka, was the apple of everyone's eye.

North of the Cardinals was the home of the Shmigelskys. Ivan Shmigelsky was on the Church Executive, and his wife, Katherine, was the hardworking *hospodynia* (chief hostess) of our Ladies Auxiliary, and according to my children, the best cookie baker in the world. Next door was Dr. Michael Buriak's medical office where, upstairs, Jimmy and Mary Chepesiuk lived. Jimmy was a city building inspector, and Mary was a most talented seamstress. Jean Harasym, Dr. Wachna's dental nurse, lived with them. Dr. Elias Wachna's dental office was four doors to the north. Dr. William Zinchesin's medical office was also located there. He had just opened his practice, after graduating in the top percentile of his medical class. Upstairs, there was an apartment occupied by Dr. Paul and Gloria Ochitwa. Then there was the Hunkewich family and then us.

My Ontario Missions

When I arrived in Toronto in 1938, there were several parishes and church families throughout south-western Ontario. Since I was the only pricst available, I travelled to them and performed the Divine Liturgy and all the necessary Holy Sacraments. These were performed in the basements of other churches, in community halls, schools, and at gatherings in private homes, as I had done in Western Canada.

During my first years in Toronto, I never sat down to one Easter Dinner with my family. After the Easter Liturgy, and the blessing of the *paschas* and baskets in Toronto, I would immediately drive to Niagara Falls, where I would do the same for the faithful who had gathered in a local public school. Then I drove to St. Catharines, where all the locals gathered at the home of the elderly Windjacks. My next stop was Grimsby, where we met at the store of the Diakowsky family. Preston (now Guelph) was next on my tour, and then finally I would return to Toronto, where the people had already gathered for Easter Vespers.

A delegation from New Toronto, headed by the Elaschuk family, came to me with a proposal. Mrs. Elaschuk was physically handicapped, but together with her husband and their two daughters, Kay and Mary, attended Services at "404" almost every Sunday. They would travel by streetcar for more than 10 miles from their home. Mr. Elaschuk asked me bluntly, "How much do you charge for services, for weddings, baptisms, and funerals?" Eighteen years of missionary service in the Church taught me to answer that I served the Lord and all people of good will. For those who can pay, I greatly appreciated their gifts of love, but those who cannot pay, I will always continue to serve them gladly, and I do not expect anything.

A few Bukovynian and Galician families invited me to an organizational meeting in New Toronto. This meeting boded well for the development of a new parish. They elected a Church Committee among themselves, and found accommodation in the basement of St. Margaret Anglican Church, where I served the first Divine Liturgy in New Toronto.

I was fortunate to have two good cantors, Michael Materyn and Semen Olynyk, to lead the responses. They would both get up very early on Sunday morning, and Michael Materyn would drive us to New Toronto, to start the Morning Service at 9 a.m. We would then rush back to Bathurst Street to begin the Divine Liturgy at 11 a.m. The faithful in Toronto began to get anxious about this *double -shifting*, because on occasion we would come back late for the Toronto Service. I called Fr. Peter Zaparyniuk, who had just come to serve the parish in Oshawa, to come to our rescue. Fr. Peter arranged to alternate Sunday Services between Oshawa and New Toronto. We now had two new active parishes *on the go.*

On the Saturday before Easter, I would also go out and bless Easter baskets in the homes of my parishioners. In each district of Toronto, up to 12 families would get together with their baskets in one house. They would network among themselves, their fellow countrymen, for this most precious and holy event of the year. Even though my load of Easter Services was exceptionally heavy, I felt that these assemblies were not unlike bringing together my church family. The families began to bond and provide support for each other. They truly became brothers and sisters in Christ, as members of a larger church family.

The $2 Donation

I often went with my father to visit a "prykhylnyk," a worshipper who had not yet committed himself to becoming a member of our church family. This one evening, my father and I sat and listened for over two hours, while this adherent talked about his views, his woes, and his excuses for not actively participating in church activities. When he was finished, he pulled out a $2 bill, which my father gratefully accepted as a donation to the church. On the way home, I asked my father why he would spend so much of his valuable time to get

such a small donation. He answered, "Today, this faith-
ful one has just learned to give. This was his first down
payment. He has bought into the family and now he be-
longs to us. He gave what he could or would. You will see
that from now, he will add and add to it, because now he
belongs." I have seen this magical transformation, over
and over, and today, the Toronto cathedral family is by
far, the most generous parish in Canada in tithing.

Every Monday and Tuesday my father engaged in
another exercise—telephoning all the people on his list of
members or adherents that he did not see in church the
previous Sunday. The conversation always started with
a concerned query, whether the absentee was ill. What-
ever excuse he heard, he always answered, "I am so
happy to hear that you and your family are all well."
Then he would add, "I will be looking forward to seeing
you in church next Sunday." For sure they came. It was
not just the recognition that they were important enough
to be called by their priest, but it showed his genuine con-
cern for them, and that they were an important part of a
larger church family.

In the farm communities, my father had used a dif-
ferent approach. There the homesteaders and pioneers
readily assembled in church. To them, it was like an ex-
tension of their home and family. They were all in the
same boat together—isolated, lonely, poor, bone-weary,
but sharing their common destiny. The cities were very

different. They were large and impersonal, and it was easy for families to become isolated and lost. My father's missionary work had to be redefined to succeed in the new environment.

Building of the Church at 400 Bathurst

By 1943, within four years of our arrival in Toronto, under the presidency of Michael White (Bily), the entire debt of $23,000 was paid off. At a very eventful annual meeting, Michael White declared that he would chair the Building Committee for a proposed new church.

All types of proposals and arguments, costs and budgets were made. Some members argued that our budget should range from $50,000 to $100,000. Some proposed that the church should look like the church, which they vaguely remembered from their village in the old country. Everyone now became an expert in church design. By 1945, Dr. Elias Wachna was elected chairman of the Building Committee, which included Dmytro Hunkewich, Andrew Oryschak, John and Theodore Humeniuk, Michael Mykytiuk, Semen Olynyk, Michael White, Nestor Hrabowsky, Sydney Kowal and myself.

After endless and highly spirited meetings, we decided upon the required parameters and set them out for the architect, James H. Haffa. The initial plans of the church were estimated at approximately $150,000. An-

Official dedication and opening of St. Vladimir Church (now St. Volodymyr Cathedral) in Toronto, Sunday, November 7, 1948.

drew Oryschak, a lawyer, and our president at that time, arranged for guarantors on a mortgage for $180,000. At a meeting with the architect, Dr. Wachna and I were told that the costs of building the church would now exceed $200,000. We received this new costing proposal from the general contractor, the Fidani Brothers. We approached William Sheridan of Sheridan Equipment, who was married to the daughter of our member, Nicholas Chrapko. Mr. Sheridan immediately loaned us $20,000, interest free, so that we could start construction.

I cannot even begin to list the many accomplishments of the cathedral parish during my twenty-five-year tenure, from 1938 to 1963 (except for an eleven-month *hiatus* during 1949-1950, when my wife and I moved to Hamilton to serve the St. Vladimir parish on Barton Street). The full story is well documented in the fifty-year-anniversary book of the Toronto parish published in 1976. I always have to give credit to the parishioners, who achieved such great success.

A Short History of the St. Volodymyr Parish

From a small group of 22 families, who greeted me in 1938, overloaded with debt, their Faith severely tested, within 26 years, by 1963, we had built a magnificent cathedral, properly adorned, with an *iconostasis* (a wall of learning or altar screen of icons) recognized as one of the finest examples of Ukrainian Byzantine art in the Western World. The membership of the cathedral grew to 770 families, and we were providing services to more than 2,500 *prykhylnyky*—families who were associated with the cathedral. In 1951, our new church became the *cathedra* (official seat) of the Bishop of Toronto and the Eastern Eparchy and blessed as such by Metropolitan Ilarion (Ohienko). Our schools now had 33 qualified teachers of Ukrainian language, history, geography and religion. We had over 400 children attending, which forced us to purchase the adjacent 406 Bathurst building to allow for further expansion. The cathedral choir became famous under its various choir conductors—Wasyl Kaspruk, Volodymyr Lach, Jakiw Kozaruk, Eugene Lazar, Michael Levak, Lev Biloshytsky, Domaty Berezenets, Yurij Holowko and Nestor Olynyk. The choir produced three excellent recordings of liturgical music.

I was first provided with pastoral assistance by Fr. Boris Yakovkevych in 1948-1949, who was later consecrated as Bishop Boris. In 1950, Fr. Dmytro Foty came from Alberta to help me with our rapidly growing church family. Toronto had become the centre of the new wave of immigration of displaced people from Europe. Fr. Foty's talented and devoted wife, Dobrodiyka Minodora, became the driving force in the development of our Ukrainian, ESL, and Sunday Schools. It only takes the right person in the right place to take over and lead to success.

We always recognized that education was to be the priority for our children. We also understood, however, that even with the highest levels of education, certificates of knowledge mean nothing without Faith. Faith works. It was in our Sunday School religious studies that this depth of Faith would be passed on to our children. Here they were taught the Commandments of God, the Holy Sacraments and our Lord's Beatitudes. The one True Commandment that Jesus taught us—to love God and to love thy brother—was the basic *ethos* of every major religion in the world.

In 1948, we held a banquet of thanksgiving at the Royal York Hotel in honour of the blessing of our new church. Over one thousand people attended, full of joy and pride of accomplishment. The period from 1949 to about 1956 witnessed a profound change in our cathedral family. Thousands of displaced people from camps in Germany, Italy, France and England started to arrive in Canada, primarily due to the efforts of Bohdan Panchuk and Dr. Peter Smylski, who saved them from being sent back to the Soviet Union. The cathedral became the focal point of arrival for hundreds and hundreds of families seeking a new and better life in Canada. We converted our new gymnasium and the auditorium at "404" into an arrival centre. Our volunteers processed each family, and attempted to find housing and care with fellow countrymen and our many church families, who opened up their

St. Volodymyr Church choir, Volodymyr Lach conductor, Toronto, 1942.

Sametz family in 1948; sitting left to right: Dobrodiyka Katherine Sametz and Fr. Peter Sametz; standing left to right: son Orest, daughter Olga and son William; absent in Ottawa: son Zenon.

homes and their hearts to their needy brothers. There was no government support for them. I spent many a fourteen -hour day helping to replace lost documents, filling out registrations and obtaining required work documents. I established great contacts with various governmental officials, who readily helped me. Their normal salutation to me became, "Here he comes again!" Many volunteers, like Myroslava Yaremko, converted their husbands' automobiles into portable soup kitchens that helped feed this multitude. Our church kitchens were always busy, staffed by our Ladies Auxiliary, who all worked endlessly and tirelessly. We also worked closely with our Ukrainian Greek Catholic brethren led by Bishop Isidore Borecky, who was my countryman from a neighbouring village in Terebovlia. Together we proved that Ukrainian brothers, regardless of religion, can set aside hundreds of years of division and animosity. This group provided our Ukrainian community with a tremendous boost of energy, wisdom, pride and direction. They were God-sent to us.

In 1954, on the initiative of Dr. William Zinchesin, we purchased a one-hundred-ten-acre farm on the Fourth Line and Dundas Street in Oakville. We arranged the financing of this purchase by finding 20 people, including myself and my two sons, to sign $2,000 guarantees at the So-Use Credit Union for the mortgage we required.

I mentioned earlier that there was an eleven-month hiatus in 1949-1950, when I spent 11 months at the parish in Hamilton. The *old guard* in Toronto began to grumble about the fast pace that we had set in the development of our church family in Toronto. They could not comprehend the vision required to build for the future in these new accelerated timeframes. Neither could they cope with the new breath of life this new wave of immigrants was providing us with. As soon as I felt that there was underlying dissatisfaction and the potential for division on the Church Council, I told them that I never had been, nor would I ever be, part of any problem for them. So, Fr. Kernitsky came from Winnipeg to replace me in Toronto, while I was assigned to the parish in Hamilton. I left behind my children in our home, next to the Church. They were grown up by now. Zenon was away in Ottawa as Deputy Minister of the Department of Reconstruction. In Toronto, William was working as a design engineer and doing postgraduate work, Orest was completing his university degree and Olga was working as a secretary and busy looking after them all.

BOOK 10

MY HAMILTON ADVENTURE
1949-1950
AND BACK TO TORONTO
1950-1963

*Take your children to church every Sunday for God
to become part of their lives and to give them purpose.*

*Teach them that when they were baptized,
their hands were anointed to do God's Work.*

Fr. Peter Sametz

A New Challenge—Again

Wasyl Festeryga, an elder, a faithful founder and secretary of the Hamilton parish, warned me, "Father, we cannot afford to pay you the recommended level of compensation as set out by the Sobor. All we have is a basement for a future church and more debts than we can handle." This story seemed to repeat itself over and over again during the years that I served the Church. I told Wasyl not to worry.

In retrospect, the 11 months I spent in Hamilton proved to be among the happiest and most rewarding periods of my ministry. The wonderful people of that city made the difference. I soon realized that I was surrounded by an amazing pool of talented people, especially an educated younger generation. For the past 30 years we had made education one of our guiding principles. Now the sons and daughters of the founders of our Church were getting established in their various professions and vocations. They truly were the fruits of our labour.

Dr. John Pylypiuk, a young M.D., offered to temporarily accommodate mother and me at no cost to the parish. Pylypiuk was holding two rooms for Dr. Morris Lazarowich, a young dentist who would occupy these rooms in a few months. I knew the Lazarowich family from Carpenter (near Wakaw), Saskatchewan. Later that summer, Dr.

Peter Smylski and his wife, Doris, made provisions for us in their home on Main Street. Peter's relatives were my *odnoselchany* (fellow countrymen) from Hleshchava. My grandmother was Anastasia Smylski, the sister of Mykola, who was Peter's father. Peter and Doris, with their four young children, lovingly made us part of their family.

The pace of my work in Hamilton seemed more leisurely, but there was no time to *sit on our hands*. Our new parish president was Dr. Stephan Klimasko, a former school teacher, who had just graduated as a dentist. Stephan was very active as a community leader, particularly with CYC, the Ukrainian Self-Reliance League. One day Stephan learned that the Serbian parish had purchased two blocks of wartime houses, across the street from where we were planning to build our new church. Although we were only using the basement of our future church for Services, I knew that there would be a need to expand. We would need a manse and space for parking. The priest of the Serbian parish was an old friend of mine from 1905-1909 at the Lviv Gymnasia, the gifted Fr. Myroslaw Podolsky. Fr. Myroslaw was a linguist, proficient in Ukrainian, Serbian, English and Yiddish. I asked him how his small parish had managed to purchase so much realty. He told me that Tom Ross, the Member of Parliament for our Hamilton riding, had helped.

I informed Dr. Klimasko that my wife and I, together with Isadore Oleskiw, our parish secretary, were all taking off to Ottawa to meet with Tom Ross. Along the way we stopped at our home in Toronto. It was after 9 that evening. My children and my nephew, John Stechishin, with his wife were having a late supper. William had just returned from an American tour with the Bandurist Male Choir where he was one of their solo dancers. I coerced him into driving us overnight to Ottawa. We arrived in Ottawa just before dawn and rested in the car until about 7 in the morning. We went to my son Zenon's apartment to wash up and have breakfast before heading over to the Parliament Buildings to find Tom Ross. Zenon was Deputy Minister of the Department of Reconstruction, serving at that time under Dr. Firestone.

First we stopped at the offices of my good friend John Decore, the Ukrainian Member of Parliament from Vegreville, Alberta (the hometown of Peter Svarich). John Decore called Tom Ross, who agreed to meet with us immediately, without an appointment. I explained to Mr. Ross that a small Serbian parish managed to purchase seven double lots across the street from our future church. I asked him to help us purchase the remaining four houses and lots. I am sure that Mr. Ross realized that I represented a parish of several thousand voters. He promised to look into this matter immediately and suggested that we seal the deal with an after breakfast toast of fine Scotch. Mr. Ross called Sam Lawrence, the mayor of Hamilton, and the mayor immediately arranged for five members of the City Commission to meet with him in his office in Hamilton. They decided that the available lots would be sold to us.

On our return to Hamilton, I called Walter Tuchtie, a lawyer, and later a judge, whom I had taught when he was 10 years old in Elma, Manitoba. Walter immediately took on the necessary legal work, *pro bono*. The problem was we needed $10,700 to pay the government for the property we had just purchased. Some members of the Church Board started to complain bitterly to the president, the secretary, and especially to me. What with the current debt load of more than $35,000 on the church basement alone, we were out of our minds to buy those additional lots with borrowed money, they said. I called my son, William, and together we put up the original deposit required to close the deal. We then proceeded to sell off three of the houses, which were moved elsewhere, and through this process we paid off all of our original costs and repaid the loan.

I recruited Fr. Wasyl Fedak, a young priest from Grimsby, to take my place. With this young and talented priest, his bright family, and the hard work of the parishioners, Hamilton became one of the largest and finest parishes in Eastern Canada.

The Hamilton parish made an astounding contribution to the proud fabric of Canada. Dr. Peter Smylski became one of the foremost oral surgeons in Canada, recognized worldwide. Peter developed the Department of Oral Surgery at the University of Toronto and became its first dean. Dr. Stephan Klimasko was also an eminent dental surgeon. Both surgeons were visionaries in the building of St. Vladimir Institute in Toronto. Stephan's daughters became violinists with the Toronto Symphony Orchestra, the National Arts Orchestra (Ottawa), and other ensembles. Wasyl Festeryga, a founding elder of the parish, saw his son George become quarterback for the Hamilton Tiger-Cats Football Club. His younger son, William, became a lawyer and was later appointed judge. Two of Fr. Fedak's sons, Eugene and Emil, graduated as lawyers and formed the legal firm of Lypka & Fedak. Later, Eugene became Regional Chief Justice of Hamilton. His son, Jerry, became a pharmaceutical company executive and Jerry's wife, Joan, a nurse and leading social activist. Walter Tuchtie, a lawyer in Hamilton, was also appointed judge. Morris Perozak, who married Stephanie Samitz, a distant Sametz relative, was also a successful lawyer and appointed judge. Dr. Morris Lazarowich and Dr. Walter Polos were also leaders in the field of dentistry and community activists.

Of course, there were many other young people who became leaders in their various fields of endeavour. I will always fondly remember the time I spent in Hamilton. The people of that city embraced me with love, as if they were my brothers, sisters, sons and daughters.

Back to Toronto

This was the first time ever that I *returned* to a parish I had previously served. The St. Volodymyr parish was growing at an astounding pace. The displaced persons—the *third wave* of immigrants—were coming from Europe. The church overflowed with worshippers. The older residents of Canada had successfully developed their own intellectual strengths with programs that the church and the Ukrainian community had fostered since the 1920s. Now lawyers, accountants, teachers, doctors, dentists and senior civil servants abounded. The newcomers had a different world view and ideological problems arose between them and the older immigrants. This had a negative effect on the unity of the parish. Fr. Franko Kernitsky spent 11 months trying to cope with this problem, but the synergies between him and the parishioners never connected, so he left to take up the parish in Windsor, Ontario.

The St. Volodymyr Church Executive was left with no alternative, but to send a delegation to Hamilton to request my return. It was the parishioners who clamoured and insisted on my return, and the Church Executive had to acquiesce. On August 30, 1950, Fr. Wasyl Fedak moved from Grimsby into one of the wartime houses we had purchased, and I returned to Toronto. I felt that I was leaving Hamilton in his good hands.

Two years earlier I had asked for a second priest to help serve our rapidly expanding church family. On December 6, 1948, Fr. Boris Yakovkevych arrived in Toronto to help. When the new parish in New Toronto, bought a hall on Tenth Street, the two of us took turns serving this parish, as well as our own on Bathurst Street. At that time, the New Toronto parish couldn't even afford to pay a streetcar fare, and I am sure this parish doesn't want to be reminded of it today. Meanwhile, the father of Fr. Boris arrived from Europe. He too was a priest and the Consistory assigned both of them to Sheho, Saskatchewan. When I returned from Hamilton, I knew that I needed assistance immediately. The Consistory assigned Fr. Dmytro Foty to help me. Fr. Dmytro was a kind and gentle man, and a great orator. He arrived in Toronto with his family from Western Canada on September 7, 1950. Together we worked through thick and thin until 1963, the seventieth year of my life, and my retirement from the parish.

My Summary Notes

The new immigrants coming to Toronto were welcomed with open arms. For almost a decade, after the end of World War II in 1945, the parishioners of St. Volodymyr Cathedral met every trainload of displaced persons as it arrived. My own car travelled almost non-stop between Union Station and the church hall. Here the sorting and networking was done to help each incoming group connect with family, friends, fellow villagers and acquaintances. Hundreds of documents had to be authenticated, proper authorities contacted and financial aid dispensed. This mammoth humanitarian task was coordinated by hundreds of our parishioners.

These newcomers were generally well-educated and industrious, and really *reached out for the brass ring* with this opportunity to restart their lives in their newly adopted and blessed country—Canada. They recognized that the churches and the schools were open to them, and they seized the opportunity to join us. There was resentment from the *old-timers* when the *new people* breathed change into our community and social life. They joined our parish, and being younger on average, and with young families, sent their children to our schools. The children numbered in the hundreds. Extra teachers were required, and they were found among these talented newcomers. The church choir expanded and cultural and social activities abounded. I once counted 26 active organizations that had formed around our church facilities. There were the dance classes of Victor Moshuk, Nicholas Worobec, Mark Olynyk, Mykola Baldecky and the two sons of Wasyl and Wira Pawluk. There were musical programs, including an orchestra conducted by John Parsons, and later the Church Readers under Petro Schkurka.

УКРАЇНСЬКА і НЕДІЛЬНА ШКОЛИ ПРИ УКРАЇНСЬКІЙ ПРАВОСЛАВНІЙ КАТЕДРІ СВ. ВОЛОДИМИРА 13/2 1955 В ТОРОНТІ.

Ukrainian and Sunday Schools at St. Volodymyr Cathedral, 1955.

The Iconostasis Building and Fund Raising Committee, 1952.
Cartoon sketches by W. Mac (Toronto Telegram).

Along with the phenomenal growth of the parish, our Church hierarchy also grew. In 1951, Archbishop Michael (Khoroshy) was appointed Archbishop of Toronto and the Eastern Eparchy. In December of that year we held the first Eparchial Conference of Eastern Canada. Our new Metropolitan Ilarion (Ohienko) bestowed the status of cathedral on our church, as the *cathedra* (official seat) of the Bishop of Toronto and the Eastern Eparchy. The first Holy Sacrament of Marriage that was held in our unfinished church was the wedding of Yaroslaw Balan, who was one of our newcomer teachers, and Anna Hryhoriak, daughter of the president of our cathedral.

In 1952, under the chairmanship of Dr. Paul Ochitwa, we contracted our parishioner, Sydney Kowal, to construct the *iconostasis* (altar screen of icons) from plans drawn up by architect Yurij Kodak, under the design supervision of my son, William, who was Kowal's design engineer at that time. John Bodnarchuk also worked for Kowal. He actually delivered and helped to assemble and install the *iconostasis* on site. That year we appointed a new choir conductor, Yurij Holowko, who set a new high bar for musicality and artistic excellence. The choir produced a magnificent recording of our Divine Liturgy together with Fr. Foty and myself.

The original gymnasium beneath the cathedral was converted for stage productions of the Folk Theatre Group under Maestro Hryhory Manko-Yaroshevych. By

The magnificent iconostasis designed by Yurij Kodak.

1953 we had built a new kitchen facility in the space between the cathedral and the "404" building. Again we called on my son, William, to engineer this project for us, *pro bono*. Our physical assets continued to grow, yet we maintained a level of debt of no more than $66,000.

In 1954, Dr. William Zinchesin purchased a one-hundred-ten-acre farm property just north of Oakville, using all the money he had in his bank account as the down payment. We then found 20 members of our parish to each sign $2,000 personal guarantees on the mortgage with the So-Use Credit Union. We called the farm the Kyiv Ukrainian Orthodox Centre. Originally, it was to be for the use of the whole Eastern Eparchy. Unfortunately,

St. Volodymyr Church choir, Yurij Holowko conductor, Toronto, late 1950s.

none of the other parishes wanted to support this project. So, the cathedral took over the property and assumed the obligations of debt. We then opened the facilities as a summer camp—Camp Kyiv. We invested by building camp barracks to house the children. Some of the children would spend the whole summer there while their parents were working. The camp was under the strict supervision of Fr. Dmytro and Dobrodiyka Foty with the help of many camp counsellors.

After the completion of the *iconostasis* we hired the finest iconographic artists we could find to begin painting the interior of the cathedral. Volodymyr Balias, Ivan Kubarsky, and Mykhailo Dmytrenko, assisted by the young Petro Sydorenko, created the interior of the cathedral that was later recognized by the Art Gallery of Ontario as one of the finest examples of modern Byzantine church art in the Free World. For many years the Art Gallery took bus tours of art students to view the art work.

One wintry afternoon Mykhailo Dmytrenko was painting the Baptism of Christ, while his young assistant stood shivering half-naked inside the cold cathedral, posing as Christ. Usually, it was Dr. Wachna, cigar in hand, who would come late in the day to inspect the progress of the work and offer his criticisms. On this particular occasion it was my wife, Katherine, who unexpectedly and unannounced happened upon the scene. She did not take too kindly to such *licentious* behaviour inside the cathedral, and let the artists know in no uncertain terms that such conduct would not be tolerated. Undaunted, the artists completed their work, and every Sunday, during the Litany of Fervent Supplication, we remember them.

In 1958, ODUM (the Ukrainian Democratic Youth Organization) moved its Ukrainian Secondary School from the Ukrainian National Home on Lippincott Street to the school facilities at our cathedral. They merged with the Ukrainian evening classes and became the Ivan Kotliarevsky Ukrainian Secondary School. William Hryhoriak became president and the parish elected three vice-presidents from the hardworking younger men, who for the past 10 years were the backbone of our parish activities. The first vice-president elected was my son William. Julian Romanko, a young successful lawyer, was elected second vice-president and Ray Mandzuk, the son of one of our founding families, was elected third vice-president. Our newcomers were also stepping up to help, like Dmytro Pryhornytsky, Dobrodiyka Minodora Foty and Mykola Kostiuk. Semen Olynyk, our long-time cantor, remained our trusted treasurer.

In 1959, we built a small chapel at Camp Kyiv in Oakville and a large swimming pool for the children. We were fortunate that we had qualified people like Murray Gaziuk (Elsie Mudry's husband), a physical education teacher and later a principal, who stepped in to set up athletic programs for our camp children.

In May, 1960, our cathedral took the initiative to organize *The Festival of Orthodoxy of Toronto*. For the first time in the history of Toronto various Orthodox Churches—Greek, Macedonian, Syrian, Lebanese, Ukrainian, Romanian, Bulgarian and Russian—gathered together for a festival concert at Massey Hall. Present were the Greek Metropolitan Athenagoras (Kokkinakis), the Antiochian Archimandrite Gregory (Abboud), Princess Helen of Romania and our Archbishop Michael (Khoroshy). My son, William, was the Master of Ceremonies and he called on the Very Reverend Semen Sawchuk (my co-worker from the inception of our Church in Canada) as the keynote speaker. Fr. Sawchuk was exceptionally well-received and his presentation *The Problem of Orthodox Unity* was subsequently published.

In June, 1963, the cathedral family gathered at a special reception to honour my seventieth birthday and my 25 years of work with the parish. I had expressed my wish to retire, but agreed to stay on until proper arrangements were made for my replacement. I insisted that Fr. Foty should take my place as dean of the cathedral, and that the parish purchase a residence for the newly appointed Fr. Yurij Ferenciw. I felt that the parish had taken enough advantage of me. From the very beginning I always had to purchase and support my own residence, but now the parish had to step up and take on this extra responsibility. Hundreds gathered for the banquet to honour me, my

Celebrating Easter with Fr. Sametz; left to right: Lesia Mucha, Helen Olynyk and little Marianne Zaparyniuk; Toronto, 1957.

wife, and my family. It was time to retire. The Eastern Eparchy had now grown to 22 parishes. Graduates of our Sunday Schools were now stepping up as leaders in various communities. In 1965, my son, William, was elected as a member of the Consistory, the governing body of our Church. He toured all the major centres of Canada with a stirring appeal for the celebration of the fiftieth anniversary of the founding of our Church in Canada. He raised over $250,000 for the Consistory, as seed money, to help cover the cost of the celebration. I remember his participation in the youth sessions—*Not By Bread Alone*. These had to be held out of doors because of the hundreds of young people gathered in Saskatoon for the celebration.

In his writings my father never refers to his phenomenal organizational abilities. He knew how to ask. No one refused his request for help or services for the Church. Although he was a quiet and humble man, he was a master communicator. With his sermons he was able to deliver the necessary messages so that everyone could understand them. Above all, my father knew he had to make the metaphorical messages of the Gospels accessible. He did not believe in the word-for-word worship propagated by the "bible-thumpers." The Gospels had to be made meaningful. They had to relate to the problems his faithful faced every day.

BOOK 11

THE SCARBOROUGH RESCUE MISSION

When you pray, you talk to God.

There is a Spiritual solution to every problem.

As children of God,
we must do things that mean something.

The mystery for us,
is to discover the real meaning of Faith.

Fr. Peter Sametz

My Short Retirement

In 1964, mother and I retired to Niagara Falls to be close to my daughter Olga, her husband Ted Bishop and their young growing family. Archbishop Michael (Khoroshy) reminded me that I was ordained to be a priest until the Good Lord calls for me, and because I was still blessed with good health, the archbishop assigned the local parishes of Niagara Falls and Welland for me to minister to. I really enjoyed serving these two small parishes. The faithful were absolutely great, supportive and appreciative. Even combined, the two parishes could not support a priest, but because I was now retired, my support costs were nominal.

As the tourist centre of Canada, and one of the Seven Wonders of the World, Niagara Falls is a magnet for visitors from all parts of the world. There were so many people that I had met throughout my life's work. Now they would visit and reminisce with us whenever they came to Niagara Falls. We would discover that I had either married them or their parents, or baptized them or their children. We were always well connected and I remembered them as an important part of my life's work.

My retirement ended about one year later. In July, 1965, the Church Council from St. Anne's parish in Scarborough, Peter Mudry, William Petryshyn, John Bodnarchuk and Peter Temrick, came to see me in Niagara Falls. They were unable to make further payments on the church mortgage to the So-Use Credit Union, the cathedral's financial institution. The unpaid interest alone had grown to over $4,500. The church was an unfinished shell with no ceiling, and the cupola had not been installed yet. They were swamped with liens by unpaid subcontractors. Meanwhile, after taking their money, the general contractor had gone bankrupt and disappeared.

All the co-signers of the mortgage were now being threatened by the manager of the credit union, Dr. Paul Kit. He told them that he had no choice but to proceed to collect the debt owing, even if it meant going after the homes and assets of the co-signers.

The Church Council of the Scarborough parish had appealed for help to the Consistory of the UOCC in Winnipeg, but the chair at that time, Fr. Toma Kovalyshyn, told them the Consistory would not be able to offer any assistance to avoid bankruptcy. Instead, Fr. Toma suggested they get in touch with Fr. Peter Sametz, because Fr. Sametz had built more than 27 churches throughout Canada during his ministry, and had the enviable record and ability to help parishes in trouble. For example, there was Ituna in Saskatchewan and Edmonton, Alberta. The St. Volodymyr parish in Toronto was also salvaged from seemingly hopeless debt. "If Fr. Sametz cannot help you," Fr. Toma concluded, "no one can!"

The "heart" of St. Anne's Parish, Scarborough, 1965.

Свящ. ТЕОДОТ ГЛУШАНЮК
Rev. Father TEODOT HLUSCHANIUK, Rector

RESIDENCE 356-d123
358-0243

УКРАЇНСЬКА ГРЕКО ПРАВОСЛАВНА ЦЕРКВА Свв. Апп. ПЕТРА і ПАВЛА

Ukrainian Greek-Orthodox Church of Sts. Peter and Paul

1906 SYLVIA PLACE,   NIAGARA FALLS, ONTARIO

3540 Gainsboro Rd.
8ᵉ серпня, 1972

Дорогі мої – Іван і Марія:

Не вибирав я собі парафії, бо хотів уже йти на відпочивок (retirement). Але, Господь ще благословив мене здоров'ям, а священиків бракує, тому я ще мушу послужити і Церкві і людям.

Я мав таке щастя, Іване і Маріє, що де громада підупадала, там мене посилали. Таке було з Велмонтоном, Торонтом, Замінтоном, з громадою св. Апп. й п. Дякую Богу, що давав мені сили працювати і в згоді жити з людьми, де оно не було.

Дякую Марії за все, що друкувала мені листи і різні повідомлення. Тепер пишу рукою, бо секретарки не маю, хоч машинка в мене є. Буду машинку ужи- вати, як почнуть рука трястися, а поки що ще здорові і служать мені.

Як маєте охоту, то приїдьте до нас на Храмове свято, котре відбудеться в неділю 16ᵉ липня. Я гарно Вас обоїх зрибітам і Івася те кож.

Остаюся з любов'ю
о. Петро з дружиною

Letter to John and Mary Bodnarchuk—"in loving appreciation."

The Scarborough Rescue Mission

I was now a *priest emeritus*, past 72. But in spite of my age, I could not refuse them. I have always had very close ties to this parish. Back in 1958, Mrs. Anna Woloshonowska called me and requested a meeting. She was living on a three-acre property she owned on the northeast corner of Morrish and Ellesmere Roads. She was elderly, living alone, and had no immediate relatives. She felt that it was too far to travel downtown to the cathedral on Bathurst Street for Church Services. She told me that she would gift her property to the Church, provided that a church be built on the site to serve the growing Ukrainian community in Scarborough.

I called Michael White (Bily), a past president of the cathedral in 1943-1945, now a resident of Scarborough, Andrew Oryschak, another past president from 1946-1949, and Dr. Elias Wachna, also a past president from 1952, to meet with Anna Woloshonowska at the home of Michael White. We accepted her princely gift and assured her that a church would be built on the site. I suggested that the church be named St. Anne's in honour of Mrs. Woloshonowska's patron saint.

I felt that the parishioners of St. Anne's would be able to handle their own financial problems. I would simply come with the Faith the Good Lord always blessed me

231

with, and help them with direction. Initially, I commuted the 100 miles from my home in Niagara Falls to the parish in Scarborough. First we started a Ukrainian School for the children on Saturday mornings. I would spend the rest of the day canvassing all of my friends, acquaintances and the faithful, many of whom had helped with the building of the cathedral.

During the first visitation by Archbishop Michael (Khoroshy), we held a fund raising banquet. I led the appeal for gifts of support with my personal cheque for $100 and I had my son, William, donate $200. The parishioners and visitors joined in and we raised enough money to pay the outstanding interest owed on the mortgage account. Within two years we paid off the original debts and started on the completion of the interior of the church. We managed to boost the membership to over 70 active member families. Our parish summer picnics became a Mecca for the Ukrainian community of Toronto.

My experience had taught me that in order to keep a parish strong and active, we had to embark upon new projects and help the members expand their vision. Truly, my Scarborough church family rose to the occasion. They treated mother and me royally. After the initial hurdles were overcome and the debt obligations paid off, excitement over the new programs and projects we had started melded the members into a great church family. I was proud of each and every one of them.

My family reunion, Scarborough, 1970.

The Very Reverend Dr. Peter Sametz, 1970.

While serving the Scarborough parish, on August 1, 1970, St. Andrew's College at the University of Manitoba conferred on me the degree of Doctor of Divinity. Subsequently, the parish held a banquet in honour of my 50 years in the priesthood.

My duties as a priest always included hospital visitations to help the sick and give them hope and prayer. For the first time in my life, I was hospitalized—with male breast cancer. I was absolutely terrified, because I knew that the illness was usually terminal. I was very fortunate to have Dr. Peter Walkovich, a famous surgeon and a member of my parish, who eased my worries and made sure I had the best care. Now I could truly empathize with the ill and the dying. The Good Lord, however, passed on me and extended my life span for many more years.

I now felt that my work for the Church in God's vineyard was coming to an end. It was my time to step aside and let the next generation of younger priests *step into my shoes*. Before we left Scarborough, I told the Church Council to build a manse for the priests that would follow, so that their families would be looked after properly. They built a beautiful bungalow on the church property.

Niagara Falls and Retirement Again!

When we moved to Scarborough, we sold the house we had purchased in Niagara Falls for our retirement. We now had to purchase another house. Within a week after we settled in, Archbishop Michael (Khoroshy) again called on me to serve the parish in Niagara Falls.

The parish in Niagara Falls was one of the smallest I had the joy to serve. The parishioners were mostly retirees with the exception of eight who were still working or involved in a business. We had a small and lively church choir under the direction of Dmytro Nahachewsky, and an active Women's Association who looked after the cleanliness of the church and its kitchen facilities. The women in our Church have always formed the foundation of our parishes.

Nearby, the parish in Welland had just built a new church, and wanted to have Church Services every week, instead of alternating with the Niagara Falls parish. I told them that I would serve them temporarily for a Sunday or two, until they would be assigned their own priest. This *temporary* arrangement lasted for another nine years.

The Good Lord blessed me with good health and a long life. He also took to His Bosom many of my contemporaries and I was left with a feeling of loneliness and isolation. I was thankful that many of their children, whom I had baptized, visited us and tried to fill this void. Mother always kept the teapot boiling, and managed a tray of something or other to treat each of our visitors. This to us was the sweet dessert of my life and it filled our lives with joy and happiness.

My belief in the ownership of land stood me in good stead. With my modest investments, we were able to sustain ourselves throughout our retirement years without receiving a penny from the Consistory Priest Retirement Fund, to which I had contributed from its inception.

I finally had to retire in 1980, in the eighty-seventh year of my life. My wife, Katherine, was terminally ill with cancer. She had sacrificed her life for our family and the church, and now I owed her my full attention and care. Although I had given my life to the Church, it was mother's strength and dedication to the family that was the true foundation of my success. I realized the depth of our love and the level of her sacrifice for our family. It was because of my family and their input that I received the love I did from my parishioners everywhere.

Why is it in life that we are ready to acknowledge our sins and shortcomings only at the very end of our lives? The defining moment seems to come to us in a flash, only when our lifespan is coming to an end. I came to this realization in time to beg my dear wife her forgiveness, and on my knees I took this final opportunity to thank the Lord for His gift of her life and her devotion to me, the family, and the Church.

Several months before she passed away, my wife and I travelled to York Cemetery in Toronto. There we both felt it would be easier for our family and friends to visit us for Remembrance Services. Katherine selected the burial plots for our final resting place. The prerequisite was that the plot have a tall Canadian maple tree.

My wife passed away peacefully, on August 21, 1982. The first *Panakhyda* (Funeral Prayer Service) was held on Monday evening, August 23, at the Cardinal Funeral Home on Bathurst Street. Four reception rooms and the hallways overflowed with hundreds of people. For the Prayer Service on the second evening, the Cathedral Council honoured her by insisting that she lie in state in the cathedral where she had worked hard to keep it spotless for many years, often on her hands and knees.

As I stood beside my father, the people came to him by the hundreds, paying homage to my mother and to talk to him. He recalled everyone by name, and remembered whether he had baptized them or their children, or married them or their parents. Only three times was he momentarily stumped for a name. It was an amazing feat of memory at 89 years of age. They had come to see him for one last time, to shake his hand, to hug him, and to thank him for his love. The funeral cortege included 70 cars. We were overwhelmed with the outpouring of support and all the cards we received. In lieu of flowers, over $10,000 was donated in mother's name, with over $7,500 donated to St. Vladimir Institute alone. St. Andrew's College received over $1,500, and more was donated to the cathedral and other charities of choice.

I Sit Down and Write

My eldest son, Zenon, had mentioned to me how, at a conference in Banff, he had tried to encourage my lifelong friend and fellow villager, Julian Stechishin, as well as Peter Lazarowich, to take the time to write their memoirs. Actually, it was my son, William, who brought me a notebook and made me sit down and write. My original writings were awkward and appeared as a précis of events that occurred in my life, or as minutes of a board meeting taken by a recording secretary. William insisted that I include as many *human interest* events that would make my life story interesting and readable. I wrote what I could recall in Ukrainian and I had Zenon translate it word for word in English.

The translations were quite stilted and had to be rewritten several times. There were innumerable difficulties encountered because both my father and my brother had passed away. The authority for the final versions rested with my father's original handwritten notes in Ukrainian. For the quotations at the beginning of each book (chapter), I selected themes from my father's Sermons, which defined each phase of his life. I realize that each chapter is only a summary of my father's life, and easily could have been a whole book in itself.

My father lived a very lonely life for two more years with only his daughter Olga and her husband Ted to care for him on a daily basis. My wife, Rose, and I visited him regularly. In December, 1984, my father suffered a debilitating stroke, which immobilized the right side of his body. It took away his ability to speak, and being right-handed, his ability to write. He could not communicate or write with his left hand. After two months of complete frustration, he bid us farewell and two days later, February 6, 1985, in his ninety-second year, he passed away.

The final prayer of our Funeral Service at interment reads, "May the lives of our pioneers be eternal in heaven, and the Canadian soil be light like a feather over their earthly remains. They will never be forgotten—Vichnaia Pamiat—Their Memory Shall Be Eternal."

BOOK 12

MY FAMILY

MY TESTAMENT

I will praise the Lord as long as I live...
The Lord will reign forever...

Psalm 146

My Family

In devoting my life to the Church, I must acknowledge the sacrifices my family made. Life is always a team effort. I was blessed with a very talented and devoted wife, Katherine, and my children, who supported, encouraged, and inspired me in my work. I am extremely proud of the success in the schooling of my children and their great accomplishments in their chosen vocations and professions. This I owe to the upbringing by their mother, necessitated by my extended absences.

Zenon, my eldest son, at age 22, had already completed his master's degree and was one of the youngest associate professors in sociology and anthropology at the University of Toronto. During the war, he was taken from the C.O.T.C. (Canadian Officers' Training Corps) to become the first Deputy Minister of Ukrainian descent in Canada. Dr. Firestone, his mentor at the University of Toronto, selected Zenon to help him create the new Department of Reconstruction, under the Honourable C. D. Howe, for planning the post-war economic future of Canada. Later, when Newfoundland joined the Canadian Federation as a province, Joey Smallwood, their first premier, selected Zenon as his special economic adviser, and made him the Deputy Minister of Community Planning and Social Development for the new Province of Newfoundland.

Zenon commented that he found Newfoundland economically like Saskatchewan during the Dirty Thirties, which he lived through, and so could empathize with their problems. After an operation for a brain aneurysm at the Montreal Neurological Institute, Zenon took an early retirement and started a second very successful career as an artist and sculptor in Ottawa. His art work was featured at art shows in Ottawa, Toronto, St. John's, and New York City. It can be found in the Firestone Collection of Canadian Art and private collections in Ottawa, Toronto, Newfoundland and Philadelphia.

In 1964 he co-authored *The Economic Geography of Canada* with Professors Pierre Camu and Ernest P. Weeks. He served as president of the Professional Institute of the Public Service of Canada, as well as chairman of the Ottawa School of Art.

Zenon married the very bright and charming Eileen Sanders, who held a master's degree in education and was a school principal. They have five lovely children— Roberta, Paul, Peter, Ellen and Jeremy, and an adopted son Stephen Duquette.

William started his successful business career, selling newspapers at Union Station and at the door of the Toronto Stock Exchange at the tender age of 13. His earnings managed to help sustain the family during our initial desperate years in Toronto. He often helped me during Church Services as my cantor during my missionary work in Saskatchewan and Alberta. I had secretly hoped that he would follow me into the priesthood, but it was not destined to be. He became a talented orator and was once described by Fr. Sawchuk's wife as *our Ukrainian Billy Graham.*

William served as a gunnery officer with the Canadian Infantry Corps in the Canadian Army. He graduated from the University of Toronto in 1949 in commerce and finance, then took a post-graduate course in engineering. After 10 years as a top design engineer of restaurant, hotel and hospital kitchens, he joined Fry & Company, an investment management firm, which formed AGF Management, where he reached the position of Vice-President of Sales and Marketing for Canada.

Apart from his business career, William never abandoned his Ukrainian roots. He taught Sunday School for 15 years at St. Volodymyr Cathedral with Dobrodiyka

Foty, and was the vice-president there in 1957 and 1958. When he moved to Hamilton in 1959 as Regional Manager for Western Ontario, he served as president of the St. Vladimir Sobor (Cathedral) in Hamilton for two terms, and was the driving force in the building of the Church School. He served as president of the Ukrainian Canadian Professional and Business Association of Hamilton, was a founding director of Hamilton Place and was awarded the Hamilton Builders' Bonnet from the Hamilton Chamber of Commerce. For 10 years, while serving as a member of the Consistory, the ruling body of our Ukrainian Orthodox Church, he chaired the Finance Committee and revamped the bookkeeping systems, managing to successfully balance the accounts annually during his tenure. Together with Fr. Sawchuk, he helped set up the Bursary and Scholarship Awards at St. Andrew's College.

In 1951 he married Rosalia Kulchyk, a beautiful and talented young court reporter, who is also a community activist. She was the first secretary of Sport Ukraina, a semi professional soccer club, and the first secretary of the newly formed So-Use Credit Union, which was set up at the cathedral. She also served as president of the Trident Chapter of the Ukrainian Women's Association.

Their older daughter, Katherine, studied piano with Margaret Parsons-Poole, Lili Kraus and Valerie Tryon and performed with Arthur Fiedler of the Boston Pops and Boris Brott of the Hamilton Philharmonic. She graduated with an honours B.A. from McMaster University and also received the Humanitarian Award. Their younger daughter Gloria also graduated from McMaster with an honours degree in English. She performed in many plays and was chosen by the Bristol Old Vic Theatre School to perform in Bristol, England, as an actress. Later, she joined a major Canadian bank and has become a prominent area manager.

Orest, my youngest son, was born in Goodeve, Saskatchewan, in June, 1928. He worked alongside William, as a *newsie*, a window cleaner, and a tobacco farm worker. At Harbord Collegiate Institute he quarter-backed the football team, and was president of CYMK, the youth organization at the Church. He graduated with a B.A. from the University of Toronto, received his C.A. in accounting, and went on to obtain his M.B.A. He started his career with the Civil Service in Ottawa, in the Income Tax Division. Later, he was chosen as Director of Combines Investigations in the Department of Consumer and Corporate Affairs. His work took him to many countries of the world. After a successful career he took an early retirement and completed his Law Degree at Queen's University. He was admitted to the Bar in Ontario as a practising lawyer. For many years he served as a member of our Church Executive in Ottawa and helped manage their affairs.

Orest married Olga Doskatch, a professional nurse, and for many years a very active president of the Ukrainian Women's Association in Ottawa. They were gifted with four beautiful and talented children. Peter, the eldest, was a brilliant scholar at Carlton University, graduating in chemical engineering. He moved to Calgary to work for a major oil exploration firm. Their daughter, Joan, graduated as a medical doctor from the University of Ottawa. Robert, my long distance runner, was awarded a scholarship at the University of Iowa where he graduated in commerce and finance. Terry, the youngest, is a good scholar and has taken on the important role of family philosopher and genealogist.

Olga, my youngest and only daughter, was the keeper of the family home. She worked as a secretary and looked after the boys whenever we were away. She married Theodore Bishop from Auburn, New York, a U.S. Army veteran who worked for the U.S. Postal Service. They lived in Orchard Park, Buffalo, Syracuse, and then in Niagara Falls, Canada, where they could be close to us in our retirement. They were an exceptional help to me, especially after mother died. Olga would come to my home every day, to help me with the cleaning, cooking and shopping.

Andrew was their firstborn. He was gifted with a quiet and easygoing nature. He graduated in engineering from the University of Waterloo and works as a construction engineer in New York City. Theodore, their second son, won the Ontario Junior Open Golf Tournament. Teddy graduated from Cornell University with academic honours in business and is the manager of a prominent golf course in Niagara Falls. Daughter Christine followed Andrew to Waterloo University, graduated in computer systems engineering, and became a star in Silicon Valley, California. She has set up master computer programs for many major U.S. corporations. She too is a fine golfer, participating in the Canadian Women's Junior Open in 1981. Michael, the youngest, is finishing high school and proficient in mathematics. He also participated in the 1982 Ontario Junior Golf Tournament.

I am grateful that the Good Lord blessed us with the greatest gifts of all—my children and my grandchildren.

Now there is a generation of great-grandchildren that is beginning to do the family proud with their many achievements.

My Living Testament

My first abiding love and thanks I give to Our Lord, who blessed me with a long and fruitful life, and gave me the opportunity to serve our people, in order to teach them His Wisdom.

My second love and thanks is to Canada, my adopted country, which accepted me as a young and eager seventeen-year-old. This great country gave me the opportunity to decide my own destiny. I enjoyed a career as teacher and educator, and was able to fulfill my divine calling to the Holy Sacrament of Priesthood.

I am thankful to all the thousands of newcomers to Canada, and to the homesteaders, who conquered isolation, hopelessness, loneliness and despair, and who showed me their astonishing strength of faith, hope and charity, while discovering the Divine within them. They came forward with their prayers of thanks for the golden opportunity offered them and their children and grandchildren. From a despised status, they established their identity, self-confidence and self-worth, and grew to become leaders of their adopted country. Their children became a Governor General and Lieutenants Governor, justices of the Supreme Court and judges at every level, premiers of our provinces and cabinet ministers, both provincially and federally, leading industrialists, teachers

Dobrodiyka Katherine Sametz and Fr. Peter Sametz, 1967.

and principals, doctors and dentists, and leaders in every other facet of the professions and vocations.

And I have a deep respect for the Ukrainian Orthodox Church of Canada. From my very first Divine Liturgy, on March 28, 1920, and my first parish, the Province of Manitoba, the Church grew to magnificent overflowing cathedrals and churches—322 parishes served by 120 priests. Bishops and metropolitans have led our Church, with Metropolitan Ilarion (Ohienko) being one of the most learned in the history of the Orthodox Faith. Our Church is in good, faithful hands and ready for the next and glorious XXI century, and the celebrations of a thousand years of Christianity in Ukraine. I leave the Church with over 150,000 members and adherents, and I will always pray, that from the sound foundation that my generation set in place, the Church will rise and take its place, quoting Metropolitan Athenagoras, "as the pristine example for all Orthodox and Christian Churches to emulate."

I leave the Church defined, as Orthodox in its Faith and Dogmas as set out by Jesus Christ, as Ukrainian in its distinct identity and heart, as autocephalous and recognized as independent and equal amongst all Orthodox Churches, and as *sobornopravna* in its governance, where the hierarchy, the priests, and the laity meet to decide the direction and destiny of the Church as equal and loving partners in a free and democratic Canada. This is the Church I leave for our children and grandchildren and all their progeny in the greatest country in the world.

I thank the Good Lord for the gift of the lives of my wife, Katherine, my children, and my grandchildren. I regarded my role primarily as a missionary priest and a teacher, rather than a theologian. I have always felt that the Divine in people's hearts was more important than strict ancient mores, rules and beliefs. I was fortunate to be a part of the growing up of Canada. I leave it to others to write the history of our Church in Canada.

Thank you for sharing my life and may the Good Lord bless and keep you, Amen.

Fr. Peter Sametz

Index

Hleshchava, UA, 19, 22, 28, 33, 36-38, 63, 208
Holovenko, 23
Holowko, Yurij, 199, 217, 219
Holynsky, Mykhailo, 185
Horodenka, UA, 157
Howe, Clarence Decatur, 118, 243
Hrabowsky, Nestor, 196
Hrebeniuk, Fr. Stepan, 108, 122, 130
Hrushevsky, Mykhailo, 27
Hrycyna, Fr. Eronim, 152-153
Hryhoriak, William, 221
Hulianaty, Mr., 158-159
Humeniuk, John, 196
Humeniuk, Theodore, 175, 180, 184, 196
Hunkewich family, 191
Hunkewich, Dmytro, 188, 196
Hupalo, 95
Ilarion (Ohienko, Prof. Ivan), Metropolitan, 116, 129, 199, 217, 251
Iliuk (Wawryniuk), Mary, 88
Iliuk, Nicholas, 97-102, 104, 108, 115
Ioan (Teodorovich), Archbishop, 131-132, 140-141, 150, 161
Ituna, SK, 93, 130-131, 134-135, 228
Ivanys, Prof. Vasyl, 184
Jasper Place, AB, 148-150, 153, 175
Jezierskyj, Fr., 20
Jezierskyj, Fr. Peter, 20-21, 28

Kaganovich, Lazar, 64
Karmansky, Peter, 52
Kaspruk, Wasyl, 199
Kedrovsky, Col. Volodymyr, 185
Kernitsky, Fr. Franko, 125, 169, 204, 212
Kharambura, Mr., 53
Khokhitva, Prof. Theodore, 184
Kirstiuk, Fr. Kornylo, 129-131, 133
Kischuk, John, 88
Kit, Dr. Paul, 228
Kitsul, Dmytro, 134
Klimasko family, 211
Klimasko, Dr. Stephan, 208, 211
Klukevych, Onufriy, 77
Kobzarov, Fr., 97-98
Kodak, Yurij, 217-218
Kokolsky, Fr., 125
Kolessa, Prof. Dr. Oleksander, 35
Kolinko, Jerry, 191
Kolinko, Katherine, 191
Konovalets, Col. Yevhen, 27
Kopachuk, Rev. Dr. Nicholas, 114
Kosiw, MB, 95, 109, 113, 119, 126, 128
Kostiuk, Mykola, 221
Kotelko family, 73, 157
Kotovych, Prof. Anatol, 184
Kotsko, Adam, 26
Kovalyshyn, Fr. Toma, 228
Kowal, Sydney, 196, 217
Kozaruk, Jakiw, 199

About the Author

William Sametz currently resides in Richmond Hill, Ontario with his loving wife of 57 years, Rosalia. He is blessed with two loving daughters, Katherine and Gloria, and three grandchildren, Alexandra and James Jarosil, and Katherine Chewchuk. William is dedicated to his Ukrainian-Canadian heritage and ever active in the Ukrainian Orthodox Church of Canada. For the past 15 years he has been Chairman of the Board of Trustees of St. Volodymyr Cathedral in Toronto. He is thrilled to have completed the book his father began writing in the 1980s.